5/20/88

To Joe Byrne,
    Best wishes to a
great Notre Dame. I hope
you enjoy this wonderful story
of the "Rock".
                Mich Bynum

ALSO BY KNUTE ROCKNE

Coaching
The Four Winners

ALSO BY ROBERT QUAKENBUSH

The Gipper's Ghost

ALSO BY MIKE BYNUM

High Tide, A Story of Class and Courage
Bryant — The Man, The Myth
Never Say Quit
Aggie Pride
We Believe
Bound for Glory
Bear Bryant's Boys of Autumn

KNUTE ROCKNE

HIS LIFE AND LEGEND

KNUTE ROCKNE
HIS LIFE AND LEGEND

Based on the Unfinished Autobiography of Knute Rockne

Updated, Revised and Edited by
ROBERT QUAKENBUSH AND MIKE BYNUM

October Football Corp.

Portions of this book have been previously published. Listed is their original source of publication:

Grantland Rice's story first appeared in his autobiography, "The Tumult and the Shouting: My Life in Sport." Copyright 1954 by A.S. Barnes & Company, Inc. Reprinted by permission of A.S. Barnes & Company, Inc.

Paul Gallico's story first appeared in his book, "The Golden People." Copyright 1964, 1965 by Paul Gallico. Reprinted by permission of the estate of Paul Gallico.

Knute Rockne's unfinished autobiography first appeared as a series of eight articles in *Collier's* Magazine. These articles, their original titles and dates of publication are: "From Norway to Notre Dame" by Knute Rockne, issue of October 18, 1930; "Beginning at End" by Knute Rockne, issue of October 25, 1930; "Four Horsemen" by Knute Rockne, issue of November 1, 1930; "Tuning up the Team" by Knute Rockne, issue of November 8, 1930; "Coaching Men" by Knute Rockne, issue of November 15, 1930; "Gipp the Great" by Knute Rockne, issue of November 22, 1930; "To Shift or Not to Shift" by Knute Rockne, issue of November 29, 1930; "What Thrills a Coach" by Knute Rockne, issue of December 6, 1930.

William L. White's story on the death of Knute Rockne, first appeared in the April 1, 1931 edition of the *Emporia Gazette*.

Jacket Cover Artwork: Dennis Luzak, Redding Ridge, CT
Jacket Cover Design: David Hirsch Design Group, Chicago, IL
Book Design: O'Rourke Graphics, Chicago, IL
Book Lithograph: R.R. Donnelley & Sons Company, Chicago, IL

ISBN: 0-945718-00-4
Library of Congress Catalog Card Number 88-90513
Copyright © 1988 by October Football Corp.

This book is dedicated to
the memory of

KNUTE K. ROCKNE
(1888–1931)

TABLE OF CONTENTS

KNUTE ROCKNE
HIS LIFE AND LEGEND

FOREWORD

Knute Rockne.

Through the years there have been many stories told about him. Some have become exaggerated or embellished while being passed from generation to generation. Others, however, have remained close to the truth.

We have all heard of how both he and Gus Dorais made famous the "forward pass" and led their Notre Dame teammates to victory against Army in 1913; and how his memorable backfield, the Four Horsemen, galloped to immortality in the early 1920s; and how he called upon the ghost of George Gipp to inspire a group of sophomores to "Win One for the Gipper" against Army in 1928; and, finally, how he reached into his bag of tricks and pulled off the hoax of the decade by dressing up Bucky O'Connor as Dick Hanley, to fill in for the injured Moon Mullins at fullback, and then stunned Southern Cal with a 27–0 victory in his final coaching appearance in 1930.

But this is the Knute Rockne which the public knew.

We, too, have gotten to know him through the years. We have listened to the stories told by our father, uncles, aunts and other relatives. To us, Knute Rockne was more than just the great football coach at Notre Dame — he was our grandfather.

The big-city newspapers often called him "the toast of Broadway," and millions of Subway Notre Dame Fans — bankers, bartenders, factory workers and little boys — adopted the Fighting Irish as their team. He only lived to be 43 years old, but in the brief time that he was with us, Grandpa gave us so many warm memories. He was a leader of young men, a builder of character and a strong supporter of academics. He also gave us a standard of hard work, fair play and fierce loyalty which we can all aspire to.

This is Grandpa's legacy. This is what we hold most dear.

After his plane crashed in the wheatfields of Kansas, the following letter was sent to Rev. Charles O'Donnell, the president of the University of Notre Dame, by one of the many people who were touched by Grandpa's infectious spirit and generosity. Of all of the letters which have been sent to our family or to the University through the years, this one is perhaps the most moving tribute to Grandpa:

Dear Father:

I feel that I must express the sympathy and the heartfelt feelings of myself and my family on the terrible loss suffered by the University of Notre Dame and the entire world in the death of Knute Rockne.

I am the father of a crippled boy, twelve years of age. He cannot leave the house and lives on the radio. He is a great boy for baseball and football, and Knute heard of him last November at the time he was most hard pressed. He wrote Eddie a letter and sent him an autographed picture of himself.

Father, when at noon Tuesday he heard the announcement over WTAM, Cleveland, that Knute Rockne was killed, he simply shut off the radio and cried; and when I came home that night he said: "Dad, the best man in the world was killed and I can't help him." Well, Eddie and I knelt down and said the Rosary for Knute, and I know he heard the crippled boy pray for him, and I know he appreciated it.

We sat and heard your wonderful sermon today at the funeral, and I am forty-six years old and not ashamed to say I cried, for the whole world lost a friend when we lost Knute Rockne. And a man who would write to a crippled boy and try to make his life happier under the conditions Knute was fighting under last fall, is a man.

Knute's picture is draped in black in my home tonight, and the kiddies all knelt before it and said the Rosary for Knute Rockne. But little Dick, six years old, said, "Dad, will there be a Notre Dame next year?" I said, "Yes son, next year and every year. Notre Dame will be there fighting with the Rockne spirit."

So, Father, when all this is over, if you see Mrs. Rockne, please tell her of Knute sending his picture to little Eddie Carty, a crippled kid out in Ohio, and that Eddie is going to pray every night for the one he calls his old friend Knute.

That was in 1931. Fifty-seven years later — and 100 years after his birth — those strong feelings are still shared by many.

John, Knute III and Nils Rockne
March 4, 1988

KNUTE ROCKNE:
AN INTRODUCTION
by Robert Quakenbush
and Mike Bynum

He was the greatest coach in the history of college football, and his name will be remembered as long as the game is played.

His players — including the legendary George Gipp and the most colorful cavalry to ever charge across a gridiron, the Four Horsemen of Notre Dame — rank among the finest and the most famous to ever earn the distinction of all-American.

His words have inspired generations of Americans to overcome impossible odds and "win just one for the Gipper."

The name of his team ranks among the six most exciting words in sports.

The Fighting Irish of Notre Dame.

His own name ranks among the most revered.

There is no argument that the most cherished symbol of the University of Notre Dame is a gleaming, golden dome crowned by a nineteen-foot statue of the Blessed Virgin Mary. It is only fitting; the University was named to honor her.

The second most cherished symbol of Notre Dame is Knute Rockne.

Those who know the University well are aware of Notre Dame's other heroes, men such as Father Edward Sorin, the French Catholic missionary who founded the school in 1842, and rebuilt it after a great fire reduced his dream to ashes in 1879. They might tell you of the morning in 1863 when Father William Corby, with his right hand raised in the air, gave absolution to the Union Army's Irish Brigade on the eve of the Battle of Gettysburg. They might point out the impressive record of leadership and public service set by Father Theodore Hesburgh during his 35 years as president of the University.

Those who regularly follow the fortunes of the University's famous football team — the Fighting Irish — might recite a lengthy litany of accomplishment. The celebrated national championships. The magnificent seven who won the Heisman Trophy. After a century of football games, the highest winning percentage in major college competition.

The Notre Dame football tradition is rich with heroic myths and affectionate apochrypha, conjuring images of gold-and-blue champions on the field of play while little blue nuns listen intently to their radios on an autumn afternoon, praying on Rosary beads for a Notre Dame victory. Indeed, the everyday lexicon of Notre Dame is a fascinating blend of words and phrases drawn from the school's three most easily identifiable traditions: Catholic, Irish and football. On crisp, clear autumn afternoons, even a first-time visitor to Notre Dame may easily explore the campus just by asking for directions to such well-known landmarks as the statue of the aforementioned Fair-Catch Corby, The Huddle, Number One Moses and the 132-foot-high stone mosaic known as Touchdown Jesus.

Young men have become legends on the football field of Notre Dame. The Four Horsemen are perhaps the most famous backfield in college football history. The inspiring story of the Gipper, in countless retellings, has become a symbol of hope for generations of young Americans who must find courage, spirit and resourcefulness in the face of seemingly impossible odds. The spirit, idealism and success of Notre Dame's Fighting Irish rank among America's greatest and most beloved success

2

stories.

But the greatest Notre Dame legend of them all is Knute Rockne, the celebrated coach who led the Fighting Irish to 105 victories in 13 seasons while establishing a shining tradition and an incredible winning percentage that may never be surpassed.

When Knute Rockne first arrived at Notre Dame as a student in 1910, Notre Dame Avenue was still unpaved. But certain elements of the famous "spirit of Notre Dame" were in place. The Notre Dame Victory March had already been composed — the song had first been performed at Washington's Birthday exercises held at the school on February 22, 1909 — and would appear to have had an immediate impact. According to the record books, the Notre Dame football team won seven and tied one later that same year.

Rockne's impact on Notre Dame was remarkable by any measure. During his 13-year head coaching tenure, which began in 1918 and ended in 1930, the Fighting Irish won six national championships and put together five undefeated and untied seasons. His teams produced 20 first-team all-America. His lifetime winning percentage of .881 (105 wins, 12 losses, 5 ties) still ranks at the top of the list for both college and professional football.

And, he won every one of the last 19 games he coached.

Rockne was the most innovative coach of his era. He was the first football coach to initiate intersectional rivalries and build a national schedule, setting a pattern that Notre Dame follows to this day. Rockne took his team, traveling by train, all over the country — from the Polo Grounds to Soldier Field to the Coliseum. Millions of Americans adopted the team as their own, calling themselves Notre Dame Subway Alumni and sharing in the joy of being Irish — if only for an autumn afternoon.

As the football crowds grew to 50,000 per game, Notre Dame's star ascended. The Rockne era brought dramatic change to Notre Dame. In 1920, for example, the school's

67-member faculty taught 1,207 students who paid tuition, room and board of about $574 per year. During the next decade, while the Fighting Irish football team won national prominence for the University — Notre Dame's faculty would increase and its enrollment would nearly triple — to 3,227 in 1930–31.

Through the years, Knute Rockne's legend has grown as his life story has been retold in one medium after another. In 1940, Warner Bros. released a motion picture, *Knute Rockne — All American*, in which actor Pat O'Brien gave a memorable performance as the Notre Dame coach. In the 1950s, on television, The Prudential Insurance Company of America (in a tribute from one great "Rock" to another) sponsored a documentary, *Rockne of Notre Dame*, as part of a CBS News series, *The Twentieth Century*, which was hosted and narrated by Walter Cronkite. Today, on videotape, images of Rockne live on in an Emmy Award winning documentary produced by NFL Films, *Wake Up the Echoes: The History of Notre Dame Football*.

There have been many other tributes to Rockne's memory. Perhaps no greater measure of his celebrity was that the Studebaker Motor Company once named an automobile after him — the Rockne. Each year, the Notre Dame Club of Chicago sponsors the Knute Rockne Awards Dinner to raise scholarship funds for deserving young men and women who attend Notre Dame. On the Notre Dame campus, "the Rock" — the Knute Rockne Memorial Building, an athletic facility built in 1937 — remains a popular place where college students and university presidents alike can play, of all things, basketball. In March 1988, the United States Postal Service will issue a Knute Rockne commemorative stamp to mark the centennial of his birth. The stamp will be unveiled by no less than the President of the United States.

Rockne was at the height of his profession during that last football season in 1930. His team had marched to victory 10 straight times — extending a winning streak to 19 games. The

4

Fighting Irish outscored their opponents 265 to 74 and finished the season with a 27–0 victory over the University of Southern California.

A few months later, Knute Rockne would be dead at the age of 43. There would be no more victories, no more cheering, and the voice of one of the most popular men in America would be silenced forever.

The great American humorist Will Rogers said at the news of Rockne's death, "It takes a big calamity to shock this country all at once, but Knute, you did it. You died one of our national heroes. Notre Dame was your address, but every gridiron in America was your home."

This book was conceived as a tribute to Knute Rockne to commemorate the 100th anniversary of his birth on March 4, 1888. As editors, we could think of no better way to bring Knute Rockne to life for today's readers than to keep our words to a minimum and, instead, include words written by the man himself and by those who knew him. Consequently, we have included material by two great writers, the immortal *New York Herald-Tribune* sportswriter Grantland Rice, who was a personal friend of Rockne's, and the distinguished *New York Daily News* sportswriter Paul Gallico, who also wrote *The Snow Goose* and *Lou Gehrig — Pride of the Yankees*. The newspaper article by William L. White (son of the distinguished editor, William Allen White), is particularly compelling. The article first appeared in the April 1, 1931, edition of the *Emporia Gazette*.

Most importantly, we have included Knute Rockne's own unfinished autobiography, which originally appeared as a series of magazine articles in *Collier's* during the autumn of 1930 — Rockne's final season. His own words tell the fascinating story of a young immigrant boy who grew up in turn-of-the-century Chicago and went on to become one of the most popular men in America.

We believe Knute Rockne's autobiography is unfinished. For although his life ended tragically in a plane crash — just months after he had coached his football team to a second consecutive national championship — his legend lives on.

For as long as the game of football is played, for as long as the Golden Dome gleams on crisp, clear autumn afternoons, the name of Knute Rockne will be remembered as an enduring symbol of victory and fair play.

February 18, 1988

MEMORIES OF A SPECIAL TIME
by Grantland Rice

Coach Jess Harper of Notre Dame took the real forward pass east in 1913. He brought it to West Point where Army and Notre Dame met that year for the first time. Harper gave the ball to quarterback Gus Dorais, who threw it to his broken-nosed roommate, Knute Rockne. Rockne caught it and Army was slaughtered, 35–13. I didn't meet Rockne on that trip. I met him some years later when I returned to the Point after he became head coach at Notre Dame.

Ring Lardner, a keen Notre Dame and Midwestern rooter, went with me on that trip to the Point in the fall of 1920. We ran into John J. McEwen, the big Army assistant coach. John J. was loaded with confidence. One of Army's all-time centers, John coached the Cadet line. Army's strong squad was headed by the flying Walter French, who earned his spurs — and an appointment to West Point — at Rutgers.

"I understand," said Lardner, "that Rockne is coming in again with that kid named Gipp."

"Who the hell is Gipp?" snorted McEwen.

"You'll find out at ten minutes to two tomorrow," replied Lardner.

McEwen did. With Army and the irrepressible French leading

17–14 at halftime, Gipp put on a second half one-man rodeo as the Irish pulled out the game, 27–17.

"How'd you like Gipp as a football player?" I asked McEwen after the game.

"Gipp is no football player," retorted McEwen. "He's a runaway son of a bitch!" One of the more volatile English instructors in West Point's long history, McEwen's descriptives remain as pungent as they are concise.

Self-reliant as a wild mustang, George Gipp came out of the iron-ore country near Calumet, Mich., on Lake Superior's Keweenaw peninsula. He came up the hard way, but at making his point on a football field, Gipp could open with sevens and keep rolling 'em. He had more than his share of speed, power, daring and deception. At times he even baffled Rock. The following, told to me by a former Notre Dame star and assistant coach, occurred during the intermission of the historic 1920 Army game.

"Being behind by three points, Rock was really laying into the boys," he said. "He had about finished and Gipp, standing nearby, asked me for a drag of my cigarette. Rock looked up and spotted Gipp leaning against the door, his helmet on the back of his head, puffing the cigarette.

"Rock exploded, 'As for you, Gipp,' he crackled, 'I suppose you haven't any interest in this game...?'

"'Listen, Rock,' replied Gipp, 'I've got four hundred dollars bet on this game; I don't aim to blow any four hundred!'"

Rock was younger then. Later, not even Gipp would have got away with it.

One of Rock's greatest gangs was his 1924 team that featured a veteran array of backs functioning behind a powerful, combative line.

In the fall of 1923, Army met Notre Dame at Ebbets Field because the World Series between the Yankees and the Giants was taking place at the Polo Grounds. I preferred the football game. That afternoon I took along "Brink" Thorne, Yale's great 1895 captain. We had only sideline passes so Brink and I watched from the rim of the playing field. In one wild end run, the Irish backfield of Harry Stuhldreher, Jim Crowley, Don Miller and Elmer Layden, swept off the field over the sideline. At least two of them jumped over me, down on my knees.

"It's worse than a cavalry charge," I said to Brink. "They're like a wild horse stampede."

That thought occurred to me a year later at the Polo Grounds when that same backfield beat Army 13-7 en route to an undefeated year, and the "Four Horsemen" emerged on my copy paper. I'm afraid it was those four football players who averaged only 157 pounds and the glory they won that made the phrase stick.

They were an amazing four men. Fullback Elmer Layden, better than a 10-second sprinter, weighed 164 and was the heaviest of the lot. Quarterback Stuhldreher, at 154 pounds, was the lightest; and the halfbacks Miller and Crowley were in between. Layden could run, block, kick and handle a forward pass. Fast and shifty, the Four Horsemen had a brand of rhythm that was beautiful to watch. They were a hardy lot and were seldom hurt. They could all block and tackle and carry the ball — the memory of them made me scoff a little during the days of platoon football, with offensive and defensive specialists cluttering up the premises each Saturday afternoon.

All were keen and smart. Rockne liked players on his squad like these four — all individualists who did their own thinking.

Jimmy Crowley was one of the wittiest men I ever knew. In practice one day, Rock said to Jimmy after he had muffed some play, "What's dumber than a dumb Irishman?"

"A smart Swede," Jimmy replied. No further conversation.

They were and are a great bunch. I'm proud to list them among my closest friends, and that's been true for a quarter of a century and more.

What circumstance brought The Four Horsemen together

under Rock? I asked Don Miller that question one day at Toots Shor's. With Miller were Layden and Crowley, three of the original four. It was a nice reunion.

"Actually," said Miller, "I didn't have much choice in the matter. My mother had sons at Notre Dame all the way from 1905 through 1925. My brother Harry made Walter Camp's Third Team as a halfback in 1909. Another brother, Walter, played in the same backfield as George Gipp in '19. I met Elmer, Jimmy and Harry for the first time when we were thrown together during our freshman year. How did you 'happen' at South Bend, Jimmy?"

"Curley Lambeau was my coach back at Green Bay High," said Crowley. "He played with Gipp at Notre Dame in '18. We were State champs and when Curley mentioned Gipp and Notre Dame...well, I was on my way."

"I matriculated at the University of Iowa first," smiled Layden. "I'd played football and basketball at Davenport (Iowa) High. But I picked up a knee in basketball. The next fall at the University, they examined the danged knee and decided it wasn't worth the gamble. My high school coach, Walter Halas, George (Chicago Bears) Halas' older brother, contacted Rockne. Rock was never too sure of that knee...but it never bothered me"...(I recalled the Yankees took a gamble on a rookie named Joe DiMaggio, knee and all, after he'd been turned down by scouts from several other teams.)

Stuhldreher played high school ball at Massilon, Ohio, the long-time hotbed of early professional football, and then finished off at Kiski Prep. Harry's older brother, Walter, was a senior at Notre Dame when Harry entered.

And that's how four Midwest kids happened to matriculate at Notre Dame. Compared to today's hunt for high school heroes, it doesn't sound like much, does it?

Compared to many of the high-speed horses galloping around big college backfields today, the Four Horsemen were pony-sized.

"If we stepped on a scale today, I don't know who'd be more embarrassed — the scale or us." cracked Crowley. "But in those days our playing weight was legit. Before the Princeton game, at Princeton in '24, Rock invited the press to our dressing room. Then he called us out. 'You've been questioning the program weight of my backfield,' he snapped. 'Here's your chance to find out...exactly.' Rock then signalled us on the scales — one by one. Elmer then weighed one hundred and sixty-one...Miller and I were about the same, at one hundred and fifty-seven, and Stuhldreher was a few ounces under one hundred and fifty-two."

"We weren't very big — then," said Miller, "just big enough. After all, Rock's entire attack was based on speed and deception — scientific football. We breathed and lived Rock's rhythm and cadence and then play execution followed. Also, we all had to block on rotating plays. No prima donnas...Rock saw to that."

"Another thing," added Layden, "Rock used to load us down with extra-heavy practice gear. On Saturday, when we climbed into game suits we felt like four Lady Godivas. Actually we were four pounds lighter on Saturday than on weekdays."

"That's right," chuckled Crowley. "We might not have been any faster but we sure felt faster...Psychologically, it was great."

It's been years since The Four Horsemen last shone as four satellites in what was perhaps Rock's greatest football constellation. I'd written countless leads before they arrived — I've written thousands more since.

"Granny," said Miller. "Rock put us together in the same backfield but the day you wrote us up as The Four Horsemen, you conferred an immortality on us that gold could never buy. Let's face it. We were good, sure. But we'd have been just as dead two years after graduation as any other backfield if you hadn't painted that tag line on us. It's twenty-nine years since we

11

played. Each year we run faster, block better, score more TD's than ever! The older we are, the younger we become — in legend. Another thing. In business, that tag line has opened more doors...has meant more to each of us in associations, warmth, friendship and revenue, than you'll ever know."

That's as nice a compliment as a fellow can receive.

Rock had another remarkable character in his assistant, "Hunk" Anderson, tougher than saddle leather at 170 pounds. A bulwark up front on the '19, '20 and '21 teams, Hunk took over the coaching reins at Notre Dame from 1931 through 1933, immediately following Rock's death.

I never saw Hunk in trouble but once, in '35 or '36. He was then head coach at North Carolina State. He was expecting a big year but his team lost steadily.

"What's your trouble down there?" I asked Hunk.

"I don't read enough American history," he said. "I thought the Civil War was over. I have an all-Southern line — good, big and fast. All my backs are from the North. My Southern line is cutting down my Northern backfield before any of them can start."

Rockne was the star between-halves orator. After one of his exhortations, Notre Dame was likely to rush out and sweep the grandstand away. One of his best was but one line: "So this is Notre Dame" — he'd say after a comparatively sloppy first half, and then leave the room. The explosive result carried the day.

Rockne's "Let's win this one for the Gipper" is ancient history. It's the kind of history, however, that American sports thrived on during an age when school spirit, college try, or what-you-will, added up to a great deal more than cynicism — which has no place in collegiate football.

In 1928, the Irish had perhaps the least successful of Rock's teams. Army was loaded with talent, depth, and most of all, a red-headed back named Christian Keener (Red) Cagle, who could handle a halfback slot on anybody's all-time eleven. The

Army coach, "Biff" Jones, a solid organizer, brought the Cadets down to the Yankee Stadium loaded for Irish.

Friday night before the game, Rock called me at our flat at 1158 Fifth Avenue, where Kit and I still make our New York home.

"Grant," he said, "the boys are tucked in for the night. How about coming down and sitting around with Hunk and me here at the hotel?"

"Better still," I replied. "Hop in a cab and come up here. Kit wants to see you. We can warm our sides by an open fire, have a spot of Tennessee 'milk' and watch the rest of the world go to hell."

That evening, sitting by the fire, Rock said he expected to be up against it — but good, next day.

"You recall Gipp," said Rock. "He died — practically in my arms — eight years ago next month. He's been gone a long time but I may have to use him again tomorrow.

"You saw Gipp on one of his better days — against Army in 1920," continued Rock — not in that staccato voice but in a quiet, hushed tone. "He fell sick later that same season. In our final against Northwestern, at Evanston, he climbed out of bed to make the trip. I used him very little that day. We were away and winging — the final was thirty-three to seven. But in the last quarter the stands chanted Gipp's name so loud and long that I finally sent him in for a few plays — on that ice-covered field with the wind off Lake Michigan cutting us all to the bone. I got him out of there, quick; but after returning to school with a raging fever, Gipp went back to his sick bed. He never got up. Pneumonia had him backed to his own goal line. He lived barely two weeks. Shortly before he went, Father Pat Haggerty baptized him into the church. After the little ceremony, I sat with him on his bed. His face seemed thinner than the Communion wafer he'd just taken — and just as white...but his forehead was strangely cool.

"Gipp looked up at me and after a moment, he said, 'Rock, I know I'm going...but I'd like one last request...Some day, Rock, some time — when the going isn't so easy, when the odds are against us, ask a Notre Dame team to win a game for me — for the Gipper. I don't know where I'll be then, Rock, but I'll know about it and I'll be happy.'

"A moment later Gipp was gone.

"Grant, I've never asked the boys to pull one out for Gipp. Tomorrow I might have to."

The following day that '28 Army-Notre Dame game played, as always, to an overflow sellout. At the half it was 0–0. The rest is history.

A sobbing band of Fighting Irish raced out for the third quarter. When Notre Dame lined up for the kickoff, I knew they were playing with a 12th man — George Gipp.

But Red Cagle didn't see any ghost as he circled deep behind his own line, reversed his field and galloped for great chunks of terrain. Cagle's runs and passes carried Army to Notre Dame's two. There, I recall, a cadet named Johnny Murrell plunged over. Bud Sprague, Army's burly tackle, missed the conversion. Notre Dame fired right back, smashing and clawing 80 yards, and Jack Chevigny rammed into the end zone crying, "Here's one of them, Gipper!" The point after was missed, and after getting the ball the Irish started another march. Rock sent in Johnny O'Brien, a pass-catching, one-play demon. O'Brien, juggling the ball as he fell, held on to Johnny Niemiec's long pass into the end zone to put Notre Dame ahead, 12–6.

Cagle wasn't through. With little more than a minute left, the Army flash gathered in the kickoff on his 10 and, circling to his own goal line, started moving. He covered 65 yards before being thrown out of bounds on Notre Dame's 35. After an incomplete pass, Cagle swept 21 yards to the 14. That was Cagle's last shot. He'd played himself off his feet and had to be helped from the field. His replacement, Johnny Hutchinson, attempted two passes, the second connecting on the 4. Hutchinson smashed to the 1-yard line but before the Cadets could fire again, the game was over.

Notre Dame carried that day, 12-6. Somewhere, George Gipp must have been very happy.

My friend Jack Lavelle, one-time Notre Dame guard, recalls his freshman year at South Bend.

"Under Rockne," said Jack, "there was a saying, 'Freshmen get nothing but abuse...but plenty of that.' How true. Some of us waited in line for three days just to get a uniform. Shoes? No matter how beat up they were, they always told you, 'Here you are, freshman. Gipp wore these!' It was a toss-up as to who wore more cleats or slept in the most inns, Gipp or George Washington. The pair I got had nails as big as shark gaffs sticking clear through the insoles. I tried to change 'em. They told me the *South Bend News-Times* was plenty thick...to make my own inner soles."

Notre Dame has long featured agile, keen, faking quarterbacks. That brings up Rock's meeting with Nate Leipsic, in my opinion one of the world's greatest magicians.

It was early in Rockne's career. He was in New York when I suggested we go to an afternoon cocktail party given by Mr. Vincent Bendix, the airplane builder, at his apartment in the Fifties. Never overly keen about parties, Rock wanted to know why we should go.

"Nate Leipsic is going to entertain," I replied. "You'll see him do some great tricks — proving again how much faster the hand is than the eye. This ought to fit into handling a football...especially in the quarterback's faking."

We went to the party. Rockne was astonished at Nate's skill. There was one trick where Rockne was given two rubber balls to handle, one in each hand. "Keep your grip tight," said Leipsic. Rock did. Then Nate waved a hand and said, "Open them up." When Rock did, he had two balls in one hand, none in the other. Rock got Leipsic to repeat this trick five or six times.

He also had other mysterious tricks repeated. "I've learned a lot today about deception in handling a ball," Rock said. "One thing I'm going to do is to send my quarterbacks to a magician. This matter of handling and faking with the ball is one of the biggest things in football...I aim to make it bigger." I can't recall a Notre Dame quarterback who wasn't a good faker. Nate Leipsic himself would have faked an opposing team out of the park.

Rockne was a man of great force, deep charm and an amazing personality. I have never known anyone quite his equal in this respect. Coaches who have been my friends include: Percy Haughton of Harvard, an exceptional coach; 'Hurry Up' Fielding Yost of Michigan; Bob Zuppke of Illinois; Fritz Crisler of Michigan; Lou Little of Columbia; Jess Hawley of Dartmouth; Dan McGugin of Vanderbilt; Bernie Bierman of Tulane and Minnesota; Alonzo Stagg of Chicago; Pop Warner of Cornell, Pittsburgh and Stanford; John McEwen and Biff Jones of Army; Tad Jones of Yale; Tad's brother, Howard Jones of Southern California; John Heisman and Bill Alexander of Georgia Tech; Bob Neyland of Tennessee; Red Blaik of Dartmouth and Army; Tom Hamilton of Navy; Frank Thomas of Alabama; Frank Cavanaugh of Fordham; Jock Sutherland of Pittsburgh; Frank Leahy of Notre Dame; and too many others to mention.

But whenever there was a gathering of coaches in any city, there was usually just one question, "Where's Rock staying?" That's where they all gathered.

There have been so many fine coaches, such great inventors as Pop Warner, Lonnie Stagg and Bob Zuppke, that no one can pick the greatest. But Rockne was the greatest of all in the way of human appeal.

I consider Warner, Stagg and Yost the advance guard of the football inventors. I think that Rockne and Percy Haughton were two of the greatest coaches, with Rockne's personality and rare human touch lifting him to the front. The man had an incisive manner of speech that electrified those around him. His manner of raising the pitch of his voice rather than lowering it at the end of a sentence was as spontaneous as it was effective. You never could misunderstand Rockne.

No, you could never misunderstand Rockne — and there's a little story behind that, too. Gus Dorais, Rock's college roommate and later his assistant, told me why.

"From the start, Rock's mind traveled quicker than his tongue," said Dorais one night in New York. Rock had been dead some ten years but to Gus, much of Rockne will never die. "Don't forget, Rock was about four years older than the rest of us when we were in school. He was always threatening to quit, but of course he never got around to it. Anyhow, in those days and some years later when he became head coach, he was a stammerer. In 1918, his first year as head coach, Rock attended an alumni dinner at which he was called upon to speak...and he stammered pretty badly. He was ashamed of himself and next day he told the Father who was toastmaster that he'd made a mess of himself. Father told Rock he had done nothing of the sort and passed it off.

"One month later Rockne had become a terrific public speaker," continued Dorais. "But there was a reason for that strange, machine-gun stacatto of his. His thoughts tumbled out in bursts...but he had to give his tongue a breather between those thoughts."

I've sat through a lot of dinners through a lot of years. In my mind Jimmy Walker was the paragon of after-dinner entertainers, but Rock was the only man who could follow Jimmy Walker. Rockne had a colossal memory. I've been with him at clambakes in some big towns where clusters of strange faces would congregate around him. He'd pick out a face in the crowd and go over and shake the fellow's hand.

"I saw you...last spring...in Atlanta...Now don't tell

17

me...It's Smith...Bob Smith...How are you, Bob?"

And Bob Smith, or whoever, would leave walking on clouds. That's one prime reason why as many as 21 special trains were needed in the Chicago railyards when Notre Dame traveled to Los Angeles to play Southern Cal. Those trains were loaded "with Rock's friends."

He was the greatest personal salesman I've known. It was small wonder that at the time of his death, Rockne was slated to take over the presidency of the Studebaker Corporation. He would have been the Eddie Rickenbacker of the automotive industry. However, where Rick is the prototype of the accepted picture of dynamic big business brass — Rock was just the opposite. His dress — a gray or blue suit — was neat but seldom pressed. His hats — brim turned up, capping a kewpie-doll skull and a bashed, pixy nose — made him an incongruous picture the first time you saw him.

I recall I was with Westbrook Pegler — who didn't meet him until Rock was famous. Peg was amazed.

"He looks like a beaten up tin can," wrote Peg.

Rockne never forgave him.

The Vanderbilt Hotel was Rock's home in New York. And whenever he was in town, his suite looked like a roadhouse. Because Rock — and Notre Dame — were on the road so much during those years, there was always a lot of baggage about. One of Rock's little tricks was to scatter rocks indiscriminately through everybody's bags. He liked to see them lug rather than carry their suitcases. He'd point to any bag and ask one of his aides to pick it up. If the fellow didn't practically lose his arm, Rock knew the bag wasn't loaded and would then take it himself.

I've been at gatherings, particularly coaches' conventions, when the noise erupting from a main room sounded like a reunion of bellowing steers. Rock, with his flair for the dramatic, usually made it a point to arrive perhaps ten minutes late. When he did enter the room the noise would throttle to a whisper. You could hear a pin drop. They'd just stand there and stare at him. Like Ruth and Dempsey, Rockne was a man of the crowd...and whatever the crowd, he was its leader.

"Whenever Rock opened his kisser," commented Harry Grayson, "the throng became silent as a tomb."

The Rockne coaching clinics — at the opening of his spring practice — had to be witnessed to be appreciated. High school coaches from all over the map would descend on South Bend thirsting for a morsel of the Rockne wisdom. I came through there in '29 and took in the first day of the clinic. Between six and seven hundred coaches were on hand. From twirling the baton to blowing the tuba, Rock was the whole show. Standing on an elevated coaching platform with his hundreds of disciples seated around him — and the Irish varsity on a nearby playing field — Rock would go into his spiel.

"Now we'll run the pass play...Marchmont (Schwartz), run that pass play." He'd point to the team and the coaches would stampede over to the sidelines...and Marchmont would run that pass play.

"Now is it perfectly clear...perfectly clear?" he would say. "Don't be bashful...This play is for you coaches...You men... Marchmont, run that pass play again!" — And Schwartz would run it, faking to this man...throwing to that one. Small wonder that practically every high school coach in the Midwest sought the personal accolade of sending a future star to Notre Dame.

The soul of propriety at various alumni gatherings throughout the country, Rock, nevertheless, wasn't against imbibing a bit. During such off-the-cuff evenings — with "practical" and important alumni making a fuss over him — Rock would at times get carried away and sign contracts to coach at Columbia, University of Southern California and I don't know where. Then he'd have to bail himself out, telling them that while his football belonged to America, his soul belonged to Notre Dame.

Saturday evenings during football season, we used to have "open house" at our apartment — with food and drink for any and all coaches who happened to be in the neighborhood. (I remember Yost used to sit there with his ear cocked to the radio trying to catch the scores despite the noise of the crowd.) Those Kaffee klatches were great fun, and many times were responsible for some pretty fair columns. Also, whenever he was in town for the Army game, Rock would come up for a late "brunch" on Sunday. In '23 and '24, he brought along his little quarterback, Harry Stuhldreher, for bacon, eggs and coffee. The recollection of Rockne's "brain" — Stuhldreher — sitting there all slicked up, his feet not even reaching the floor, is a picture that Kit and I treasure.

During Rock's thirteen years as head coach — from 1918 to 1930 — years when Notre Dame picked up followers by the millions, the Rockne System became the great vogue, from Yale to St. Mary's. The more the Irish won, the greater became Rockne's vision of not only giving Notre Dame spectacular seasons but of giving his alma mater the Number 1 place in the football world.

Rockne took his teams far and wide, seeking the intersectional powerhouses of the country. At West Point; Atlanta, Georgia; Princeton; Lincoln, Nebraska; Palo Alto; Chicago — wherever Rockne went — he was a Pied Piper picking up followers by droves. In that way the teams of Notre Dame became the teams of the people, and Rockne became football's personal trademark for some 30,000,000 fans throughout America.

I saw Rockne at New York's Polo Grounds in December 1930. Phlebitis had claimed his once swift legs. Muffled in a blue blanket, he was wheeled into place beside the bench of the Notre Dame All-Stars, who were playing the New York Giants in Mayor Jimmy Walker's answer to the depression. The game, played for the relief of the unemployed, was a pushover for the

Giants. Benny Friedman had a field day with his passes and the Owen brothers, Steve and Bill, had a huge barn party in the line. Several of Rock's old stars, Jack Cannon at guard and Adam Walsh at center, along with graduating Frank Carideo at quarterback, played some great football. However, brought together from the four points of the compass at the last moment, they simply were no match for the Giants.

The following day Rock and I had lunch together at the Park Lane Hotel. Despite the condition of his legs, he moved pretty well and seemed in good spirits. Hollywood wanted his technical direction for a football picture, and he wanted me to write the script. I agreed.

"We ought to make it next spring or early summer. It'll take only three or four weeks. I'll go out there sometime this winter to get things in order."

"All right, Rock," I said…"and good luck."

I believe that's where Rock was heading when his plane, carrying a half dozen other passengers, crashed in a Kansas cornfield on March 31, 1931.

On the afternoon of Saturday, April 4, a vast assemblage of people from every walk of life gathered at Notre Dame to pay their last respects. They were all there, from the butcher's boy down on Main Street to the personal representative of the King of Norway.

Rock's last team carried him to his grave, near his beloved university, beneath the great branches of a gigantic oak. Knute Kenneth Rockne, an Olympic personality in American football, had barked his last command.

HE WAS THE TOAST
OF BROADWAY
by Paul Gallico

If you are interested in the passage of time and the changes it brings about, you have only to glance at the photographs of the football teams of the 1900s and those of today and, if nothing else, note the difference in attire and armor plating.

Our forefather, his hair neatly parted in the middle, wore short pants known as "moleskins," either quilted or with some sort of ribbed stiffening in them, a woolen jersey, and over it a kind of leather jerkin. Underneath was a device of leather called schimmels, that laced across the shoulders, to protect the collar-bone from breakage. The helmet, if and when worn, was of soft leather and covered the ears. Some players used a rubber noseguard.

Compare this mild sort of padding with the almost rigid armor worn today and in particular the solid, rock-hard, plastic helmet with its steel projections.

The uniforms have altered, as have the size and shape of the ball, and the rules of the game itself have been changed incessantly, to the point where a veteran of the year 1900 might not understand the play of 1965 unless an interpreter were at hand to explain it to him.

It was during that famous decade of 1920 to 1930 that football underwent possibly its greatest transition from old-fashioned to modern.

But it was also during that period that a brand-new phenomenon appeared in American football and one which has all but disappeared today. It developed a nationwide emotion that before the decade was out had become almost religious in its nature, and Knute Rockne was its high priest.

At this extraordinary time in the history of American sports as well as that of the people of the United States, Knute Kenneth Rockne, football coach of Notre Dame, was himself a most prodigious, phenomenal, and singular person and more than any other, directly responsible for the extent and violence of the spirit that infected the game and spread to the farthest corners of the country. For ten years this bald, round-faced man with the squashed-in nose and his sensational teams, each fall, initiated a six-week emotional binge among fans, but particularly involving heretofore non-fans of the game of football, that amounted almost to the hysteria of evangelism.

Prior to this, football player Joe College was something of a comic figure with his turtle-necked sweater, Buster Brown haircut, flying wedge, and determination, if need be, to "Die for dear old Rutgers," to the accompaniment of a chant of "Rah-Rah-Rah, Sis Boom Ah" from the crowd on the sidelines, to stimulate him to the sacrifice. Mass cheering has survived in modern football, but it is today nothing but a spectator catharsis and is considered a nuisance by the player who has business to get on with and signals of logarithmic complication to remember and transmit in the pre-play huddles.

Early interest centered around the Big Three, the Universities of Yale, Princeton, and Harvard, but the crowds attending their annual titanic clashes were composed of alumni and their families. Considering the enrollment of these universities, graduating hundreds of nubile young men every year, it did not take long for them to breed pennant-waving partisan and vociferous audiences for these contests. There might be a few outsiders, ambitious youngsters of the ever-increasing middle class, who hoped someday to attain university status, who were "for" Yale or "for" Harvard, but by and large the rivalries between these great seats of learning were family affairs.

Newspapers in the East were beginning to give publicity to the annual games involving the three, since many of their readers were connected in one way or another as partisans of the universities. Socially the Big Game was a wonderfully gay and youthful affair, featuring the prettiest girls in the world decked out in chrysanthemums and bright ribbons, accompanied by handsome, coonskin-coated young men, bearing pennants showing the names and colors of the universities and with flasks on their hips since Prohibition was with us. These clashes often coincided with the Thanksgiving festival; November winds brought carmine to fresh, young faces; young hearts, particularly feminine ones, beat high, and on the field below, twenty-two heroes patriotically and chivalrously battled for the glory of alma mater and the admiring glances of the little beauties in the stands.

The man in the street, however, largely ignored it. The hullabaloo struck him as juvenile, the game of football itself as faintly ridiculous, with its pushing and shoving and piling up, and there was still largely the situation of town and gown; the self-made man versus the college smartie. It was Knute Rockne, in the main, who brought about a drastic change in the situation.

Neither a born American nor an Irishman, nor a Catholic, until toward the end of his life he became a convert, he was the coach of the University of Notre Dame, located at South Bend, Indiana; a Catholic university and a stronghold of Irish Catholicism in the Middle West. It was the semi-religious background of this school which lent just that touch of mysticism and emotionalism as a starter. But all the rest of the extraordinary spirit and hysteria which marked so many of the games played by Notre Dame during that decade were supplied by Rockne.

The sentimental jag reached its high point in the month of November before, during, and after the annual contest between Notre Dame and the Cadets of the United States Military Academy at West Point, played in New York City; an affair which took on almost the quality of a pagan autumnal rite, and engaged the passionate observation of millions of people.

You will see if you look at photographs of the early Notre Dame teams which first came to New York, that their costumes and headgear are old-fashioned, somewhat between the earliest uniforms and the modern. But there is something equally old-fashioned belonging to that era of the twenties that doesn't show up in pictures. It is the aura of dedication that was quite different from anything one seems to feel or experience about football and its participants now, except perhaps, curiously enough, in the ranks of the professionals and their adherents. It is the pros and their fans who, by and large, have taken over the fervency that used to attend the college games.

That difference, I am convinced, was supplied by one man, this same Knute Rockne, himself a football star of Notre Dame from 1911 through 1913 and head coach at the university from 1918 until his tragic death in an airplane crash in 1931.

He was a hired hand, engaged like so many others to teach the sport to university students, train and advise them, prepare them physically as well as spiritually and strategically and turn out winning teams if possible. But more than any other in his profession he captured the hearts and imaginations of the Americans of his time.

He was responsible for many strategic innovations in football play, such as the shift and dramatic use of the forward pass that opened up the attack and made it more visual. But it was for quite a different contribution that he made his major impact upon both his day and the game.

He brought an extra dimension to football and in particular to the teams he coached, which enabled the spectators to share in the emotions engendered by the struggle on the field far more than they had ever done before.

American college football was a battle which very often transcended not only itself but those participating in it as well, to the point where suddenly the onlooker saw it no longer as a spectacle provided by two sets of young men, but rather as a giant and abstract manifestation of two contending wills. If offered a phase of the classic physics paradox of what happens when an unstoppable force encounters an immovable object.

Further, unlike other sports, there were no villains in these college clashes. The teams were too ephemeral, here one year, graduated the next. Partisanship was a matter of adherence to a university rather than individual members of its football squads. Outstanding stars achieved tremendous followings, but whoever heard of hating a halfback or an end?

And finally, there was another kind of sharing for which Knute Rockne was responsible, since it was his teams that sent the renown and name of Notre Dame soaring. It took the form of the famous assistant Irish and Subway Alumni of the South Bend institution, whose headquarters were in New York, but whose members were scattered to the four corners of the land wherever there was anyone named Ryan or Rafferty, Clancy or O'Houlahan; or Kraus or Cohen or Tony Bacigalupo.

This was quite one of the most amazing phenomena and transitions of the times. Suddenly everybody wanted to get into the act and belong. Hundreds of thousands of people prior to this time who had looked down upon the game as "Rah-Rah" stuff now wanted to identify themselves with it, an identification, incidentally, far more rabid and partisan even than that exhibited by the alumni, or family members of universities.

Dates and facts here become a matter of some importance. The initial Army-Notre Dame meeting took place at West Point in the fall of 1913. Up to that time few had ever known Notre Dame in the East. The Westerners won 35 to 13 and from then on one heard plenty about the Catholic school.

One of the players on the Notre Dame team of that year was an end by the name of Rockne, another was a young back, Gus Dorais. The Notre Dame coach was Jess Harper. For the first time experts in the East saw the forward pass — mostly Dorais to Rockne — used as a part of sustained offensive football rather than a last-minute desperation. Overnight it seemed that the game had been opened up, revolutionized, and turned into a thrilling and dramatic spectacle, no longer dependent upon partisan loyalties for thrills. It had become something to watch. But the Subway Alumni were not yet.

In 1918, Knute Rockne was appointed head coach at Notre Dame and his team sported a respectable 3-1-2 record. Subsequently in 1919 and 1920, his teams were Western champions and national champions, winning a total of eighteen games and losing none.

From 1921 through 1930, Notre Dame won eighty-four, lost eleven, and was tied three times.

The man behind this fantastic string of victories was this same Rockne, and West Point and Notre Dame acquired the greatest rooting sections in the history of the game. Only seventy thousand at a time could crowd into Yankee Stadium in New York actually to see them play, but millions became fanatical adherents via the radio and the newspapers. The game of football — at least this particular one involving Army and Notre Dame — had broken through every class barrier that still existed in the United States.

World War I had supplied a new and ready-made cheering section for the two service teams. If during our brief embroilment in that catastrophe you had worn khaki, you were for Army; if bell-bottomed trousers, Navy was your team from then on. The annual clash between Army and Navy took on an importance it never had before, far transcending even the game between Yale and Harvard, for now we had alumni, if not actually of West Point or the Naval Academy, at least of the two services. But until the advent of Notre Dame there was no school which extended a mass appeal to ordinary civilians.

With the sky-rocketing of this university out of the West, their brand of exciting, razzle-dazzle, wide-open football, the wonderful sobriquet of "Fighting Irish" pinned on them by the sportswriters (in spite of the fact that the majority of the names of the team members were not Irish — of the thirty letter-winners in 1927, for instance, only seven could be said to have monickers stemming from the Ould Sod), everything changed. The warm affection and the curious kind of sports love engendered by the unique personality of Rockne led literally millions of people who had never been to college or seen a campus to adopt Notre Dame as their very own and thereafter identify themselves with the school.

Beginning with 1923, New Yorkers had the opportunity of seeing this team in action, provided they could buy their way into the baseball parks. That year the Army-Notre Dame tussle was played at Ebbets Field in Brooklyn. In 1924 and 1925, fifty-five thousand souls jammed the Polo Grounds beneath Coogan's Bluff. From then on it was seventy thousand persons packing every nook and cranny of Yankee Stadium.

New York was never before, or since, so sweetly gay and electric as it was when Rock brought his boys to town; the city was wild with excitement and filled with pretty girls and gray-clad Cadets who thronged the hotel ballrooms when it was over, while the civilian fans argued or battled it out in the Third Avenue speakeasies.

These Interborough Rapid Transit Notre Damers came from every walk of life; Gentile and Jew, Broadway show-biz and nightclub dolls, bartenders, prize fighters, cab drivers, bookmakers, delicatessen store owners, denizens of the half as

29

well as the whole underworld, rich man, poor man, beggarman, thief — and, of course, the Irish.

For a nickel train ride, a scalper's price of admission, and two bits more for a feather, or a banner, they became faithful and fervent rooters. They felt that they belonged, and that the wonderful bizarre and romantic mantle of Irishness was spread over them. A large portion of them were no more genuine Hibernians than were those members of the Notre Dame squads whose names ended in "ski," "berger," "isch" or "vitch," but it made no difference to the self-appointed alumni. Once they had decked themselves out in the Notre Dame colors, predominantly green, naturally, their identities were merged with those extraordinary football wizards from the West.

The very fact that this squad came from that part of the country and the never-before-heard-of town of South Bend, lent added mystery and fascination. There were some pretty good football players and teams around the East at that time too: Syracuse, Colgate, Cornell, Pennsylvania, not to mention the Big Three — Princeton, Harvard, and Yale, as the game developed. But when the brilliant and winning "Irish" arrived, the masses ignored the local squads, allied themselves with the strangers, and took them to its collective heart. In the mongrel mixture of the melting pot, all became Irish and "Fighting Irish" as well.

When the November sun had set behind the Polo Grounds or Yankee Stadium, and the Notre Dame eleven had quit the gridiron with the football and the winning score, it would be these same bartenders, bookmakers, shopkeepers, nightclub doormen, and Broadway bums who would flood onto the field and begin rocking the goalposts to bring them down, cart them off, and carve them up into souvenir splinters to be carried thereafter as talismans of the luck of the Irish.

One famous backfield of those days was most felicitously named "The Four Horsemen" by star sportswriter and poet the late Grantland Rice. He took the name from the Ibanez novel and moving picture: the Four Horsemen of biblical lore, Famine, Pestilence, Destruction, and Death, and this kind of publicity and dramatic buildup was on a par with that which was greeting heroes and millionaires in other big-league sports. Cash began to flow into the coffers of university athletic associations as never before.

But if, as noted, players were somewhat ephemeral — three years saw them graduated and replaced by others — one gigantic figure remained, the high priest of those football days and the idol of not only small boys, but adults as well, and that was Rockne himself. He had magnetism to burn and that indefinable champion's touch, that intangible something that inspired not only his players, but reached beyond them to the lowliest self-appointed Subway Alumnus who loved and rooted for "Kanute Rockne of Noter Dame's Fightin' Irish." Dempsey had it, Tunney had it; so did Johnny Weissmuller, Tommy Hitchcock, Earl Sande, Bobby Jones, the Babe, Red Grange, champions all. When they came into a room, you knew they were there. Wherever and whenever Rockne appeared there was no doubt as to who was the star of the show.

There were many other great football teachers in that era, contemporary with him: Pop Warner, 'Hurry-Up' Yost, Amos Alonzo Stagg, and Percy Haughton, but none of them had that extra, star quality that Knute possessed and the ability so to fuse eleven men into a unit representative of his own peculiar and often impish spirit. His teams sometimes played football that had a definite tinge of humor, because Rockne was a gay, witty man, and made his practice sessions light-hearted and enjoyable. And this, too, managed to communicate itself to us.

Coaches are often overrated. After all, it is the boys who get out onto the field, take the knocks and carry the ball. But every so often a genuine colossus appears whose influence and teaching cannot be underestimated, and Rockne towered head and shoulders over the best of his profession. He took four of the worst freshman bumblers ever seen falling over their own feet, or running into one another — Miller, Layden, Stuhldreher, and Crowley — a quartet of totally different characters and temperament, and within a year welded them into the greatest backfield combination ever seen on a football gridiron up to that time. These were Grantland Rice's famous "Four Horsemen" who flourished in 1922, 1923 and 1924 to tie Army once and beat it twice, winning the national championship in their final year, and concluding with a 27–10 win over Stanford in the Rose Bowl, a record of ten won, none lost, none tied, against such opposition as Army, Princeton, Georgia Tech, Wisconsin, Nebraska, Northwestern and Carnegie Tech.

The Four Horsemen passed on. Notre Dame continued to win. Others, too, could play the Rockne brand of football and react to that irresistible fascination. It was not until after 1931, when this great coach died, that his accomplishment became apparent in the university's won-and-lost column. Rockne's overall record as Notre Dame coach, starting in 1918 and continuing through 1930, was: 105 won, 12 lost and 5 tied. He fielded five undefeated and untied teams. Two decades later another Irish coach, Frank Leahy, ran up a string of thirty-nine consecutive victories. But that was later — much later. It was Rockne who broke the ground and taught his boys the best and brainiest football that had been seen up to his day, and then fired them up to play it beyond anything that had ever been experienced before.

How was this accomplished?

It was again the combination of the times, the psychological climate, but above all the man. For over and beyond the personality of Rockne, pumped up by the publicity flacks of Notre Dame, and believe me there was some pumping, there was a genuinely unique individual. In the games played by Notre Dame under Rockne, and in particular those classics against Army, there were some brand-new elements introduced: humor, affection, and a curious kind of sports love that manifested itself in odd ways.

Notre Dame played hard, rough, out-to-win football, but many of their players were witty and great kidders and often put their opponents out of stride with their sallies. The team spirit of these boys was tremendous. They sacrificed and blocked for one another, fought for one another, but in a strange way they loved their enemies too, and could be chivalrous because their coach was a chivalrous man.

Earlier, when Army was playing Notre Dame at West Point, Rockne's version of the shift was throwing the soldiers badly off balance, instigating complaints that it was an illegal maneuver.

It was not actually so, for Rockne never played illegal football, but after the first half Referee Tom Thorpe said to Rockne, "I just don't know what to do about that shift of yours, Rock. The Army is on my neck that it's illegal. I know it isn't, but it's so close that it's difficult for anyone but an official to judge."

Rockne said, "All right, Tom, I'll tell you what we'll do. We'll play the second half without the shift."

They did and scored the same number of touchdowns as in the first half.

This was the kind of story which appealed so strongly to the people we were then.

Rockne was a very moral man and we were just emerging from a period when morality was still adjudged a virtue. An ebullient substitute scored a touchdown, and as he raced across the goal line, he raised five fingers to his nose and cocked a snook at the pursuit. Rockne yanked him and took his suit away.

He was moral in the sexual sense, another characteristic of an era which once denied entrance to a European countess on the grounds of "moral turpitude" because she'd had a boy friend. He closed down a *maison de joie* known as "Sally's," above a feed store on LaSalle Street in South Bend, as having a deteriorating effect on the neighborhood. The police dragged their feet when requested to cooperate, since apparently some kind of profit-sharing plan was in operation. When repeated appeals failed, Rockne made another suggestion. Either Sally's closed, or he would bring his football team down and take the place apart. The threat of this kind of publicity shook the city fathers to the soles of their shoes, and Madam Sally's establishment took over premises in another town.

Rockne was known for his psychological warfare and the sentimentality of his dressing room pep talks, two of the most famous of which are revealing. In one, after his team had taken a first-half shellacking and sat waiting for the blast, Rockne merely poked his head in the door of the dressing room and remarked quietly, "Oh, excuse me, ladies! I thought this was the Notre Dame team." He was a master at reducing swelled heads, and when his Four Horsemen had an off day, he would suggest that they carry their press clippings onto the field with them and read them aloud to the enemy.

Another famous dressing room oration concerned the plea from the dead — "Go out and win this one for the Gipper, boys!"

According to the legend, George Gipp, probably the most celebrated football player ever developed at Notre Dame and coached by Rockne, lay on his deathbed from pneumonia brought on by overindulgence in all manner of things, and dying, is supposed to have said to Rockne, "If you ever need to win one badly, ask the team to go out and do it for me," etc., etc. The whole thing sounds apocryphal, but quite classical for our times and the kind of treacle we loved to swallow. Actually, the real deathbed story was quite different. Rockne, holding the boy's hand, said, "It must be tough to go, George," to which Gipp replied unequivocally, "What's tough about it?"

At any rate, it was currently acknowledged that Rockne had used the "Win this one for Gipp" plea and the boys had come through.

What was not common currency was that George Gipp, in addition to being a brilliant football player, was a very bad little boy. He was everything that a Notre Dame college boy ought not to be — a womanizer, a pool shark, a card player, a gambler, and a drunk, and Rockne was attached to him. And with this love for a sinner who could deliver the goods on the football field, any phonyness in Rockne's morality falls away and he stands exposed to us as a genuine human being.

The story of how Gipp was able to place a wager, an act which today would have gotten him disqualified not only from amateur but from professional football as well, is even better. He had "agents" who did his betting for him, and they reported that for the Indiana game at Indianapolis, the gamblers wanted no part of Notre Dame or brother Gipp. The "agents" were planted in the local betting emporium where, the night before the game, a tall, muffled figure with his overcoat collar turned up, marched in and shakingly demanded a Bromo Seltzer, in those days a popular cure-all for hangover. He shivered, and with trembling fingers raised the glass to his lips, swallowed, coughed, gagged, and finally after downing it, staggered out of the door. Someone asked, "Who the hell was that wreck?"

Here, an "agent" volunteered the reply, "Why, don't you know? That's George Gipp. He's been like that just about all week. I doubt if he'll get into the game at all tomorrow. It won't even be a contest without him."

The whole thing, of course, was an act. Gipp hadn't had a drop, got his bet down, and collected the money.

The Gipper could make a living out of pool room hustling and did. He bet heavy sums of money on the games in which he played and spent more time carousing in off-limit South Bend hangouts and saloons, and card-playing, and eventually he was expelled from Notre Dame. But upon Rockne's plea and the passing of a stiff oral examination, he was readmitted.

The friendship between the nineteenth-century-type tough-guy Americano and the soft-spoken, twentieth-century Rockne was the stuff of which our stories were made.

Rockne had the ability to associate names and faces and remembered hundreds upon hundreds of boys. One of his old students recalls the day when nearly six hundred boys went out for freshman football. Rockne divided them into eleven sections, in accordance with the positions they said they played. When these formed groups, Rock asked each one his name. The following day, when they assembled, Rockne had them form a huge circle, and without notes called out every one of them by name and assigned him to the proper assistant coach.

Five days a week between twelve-thirty and one o'clock in the afternoon, in the basement of the old library building, Rockne conducted skull practice in a football clinic. He and Hunk Anderson would pose hypothetical problems of rules and situations and ask for solutions, and it was through these sessions that Notre Dame players acquired such a knowledge of every aspect of the game that they were able to take advantage of any situation which might develop on the field.

Small boys hanging about Cartier Field got into the second half free, until the empty seats were filled. But there were some who passionately wanted to see the first half as well. In those days members of the team ran from the locker rooms onto the field swathed in blankets, and it was not unusual to spot two big cleated feet under one of those coverings surrounded by four, or six, smaller feet, trying to keep in step. Rockne would never see this. Some of these stowaways later became Notre Dame stars themselves.

He was a brilliant raconteur and was in tremendous demand at Rotary luncheons, Lions Club dinners, or any large stag function where men got together to feed and listen to after-dinner speeches.

Added to all of this was the fact that the public at large believed him to be something of a wizard, for there certainly seemed to be magic connected with his successes. Everything he touched turned to gold. He wove his spell over his own players and produced strange miracles, such as the time Adam Walsh, his all-America center, once played the entire last half of a game with two broken hands. But what were crippled digits compared to love of Rockne and the determination not to let him down? Not a single bad pass was charged against him through this whole agonizing half.

Knute's influence extended not only to his own squad, but during his all-too-short career as a coach, many hundreds of thousands of other young men warmed their own competitive spirits at the bright fire of this man who stood for everything that was right, good, and successful in American sports of his era.

All this, of course, led to the cult of Rockne. Just as the melting post of Assistant Notre Damers and hoi polloi alumni attached themselves to the Notre Dame team, so Rockne became their Shaman and High Priest, and was worshiped, back-slapped, and adulated wherever he went. The phenomenon was unique. Much of the fame of Notre Dame of today rests upon his shoulders, because of what he did and was.

And withal, just like with the other great champions who populate this volume, even though you collected and enumerated their extraordinary qualities, skills, and abilities, there was still that mysterious intangible that made them into these special people.

The record of Frank Leahy in the decade 1940 through 1949 was hardly less than that of Rockne. But there was no Leahy cult that I can remember. He was simply a popular, successful coach of a famous university. It was Rock the pioneer who had that extra-added, super champion quality which was unforgettable. I can see him still today, with his squashed-in nose (from baseball, incidentally), jug-handle ears and humorous mouth, striding the Notre Dame sidelines during a game, or deep in conversation with his second-in-command on strategy as the pattern of victory or the threat of defeat began to emerge upon the gridiron. His presence made itself felt. Eleven young men on the field running, kicking, passing, and carrying the ball, but behind them was Rockne.

For all that, the man was no paragon or goody-goody, nor was he faultless. He made mistakes but he never lacked the courage to face up to them and admit his errors. He could apologize to the world or to the most humble freshman candidate. But his faults fade into insignificance today beside the memories of his towering character and ability.

At forty-three his life came to an end, far too young, when on a flight to the West Coast from Kansas City, his plane crashed into the Flint Hills in a fog. Perhaps a character so unique and adulated was fortunate to quit the scene at his peak. Certainly his passing marked the end of that particular football era with its newborn excitement. It is all different now.

THE
UNFINISHED AUTOBIOGRAPHY
by Knute Rockne

A YOUNG BOY'S DREAM

The first time I learned a football was not only something to kick, but something to think with, was when I saw a great football player in action for the first time. A sandlot youngster, who regarded football as a pleasantly rough recreation, I had no hero worship for any player and no interest in any team. But when the Eastern high school champions of 30 years ago challenged the Western champions, the meeting of the two teams in Chicago was a great event.

Brooklyn Prep was the Eastern outfit and Hyde Park High in Chicago the Western. Crashing the gate — a habit of mine as a youngster — I sat spellbound through that game. It was one-sided; the final score was 105 to nothing in favor of the Chicago team.

But the clearest picture remaining from that slaughter was not the overpowering might of the Western lads, who had among them the famous Hammond brothers, later Michigan stars. The striking feature was the brilliant, heady play of Hyde Park's quarterback — a lad named Walter Eckersall. He played prairie football — mainly wide sweeps around ends — but by instinctive timing he hit the heavier Brooklyn linemen until they were dizzy. With no more than four fundamental plays he worked so

41

quickly and coolly that he made his offense bewildering.

Eckersall's sharp staccato calling of signals, his keen handsome face and the smooth precision with which he drove and countered and drove again, handling his players with the rhythm of an orchestra leader — all this gave football a new meaning to me.

After the game was over and the Western boys went cheering from the field, shouting the name Eckersall like a slogan over the defeated Easterners, I tried to get close to the hero of the day. Two or three thousand other youngsters were trying to do exactly the same thing, so I had to go home without a handshake — yet, for the first time in a young and fairly crowded life, I went home with a hero. Dreams of how, some day, I might shine as Eckersall had shone that afternoon, were my lonesome luxury. For years they were nothing but dreams. Eckersall went on to greater glory as the sensational star of the University of Chicago. My path took me from high school to nothing more athletic than being a mail dispatcher working nights, for years.

But there came an afternoon when the Notre Dame squad ran on to a Chicago field with the former sandlot boy, ex-mail dispatcher, as captain. The referee was Walter Eckersall. In his smart white togs, he looked scarcely a day older than when he led Hyde Park in its overwhelming victory over Brooklyn. Grasping his hand, I said, "I've been waiting years for this."

"For what?" said Eckersall.

"To shake your hand," I said, recounting how his brilliant performance for Hyde Park High had turned my mind seriously to football.

"Stop, stop," said Eckersall in the middle of the recital, "or Notre Dame will be penalized 5 yards for speechmaking."

How a youngster from Voss, a hamlet in Norway that lies between Bergen and Oslo, could find himself in his mid-20s captain of a typical, Midwestern American football team may require explaining. Perhaps it's sufficient explanation to say that this evolution is a typical American story — in business, athletics and politics. It has occurred so often that it's ordinary. The breaks came my way when I had sense enough to take them, and while that's an unromantic way of explaining a career, it has the advantage of being the truth.

Her celebrated majesty, Queen Margaret of Norway, had something to do with it. At least, there's the word of a student of Norse genealogy to that effect. It's on an elaborately inscribed piece of parchment that looks like a map-outline of all the football plays ever invented. This, on close perusal, informs me that I'm descended — among others — from one Enidride Erlandson of Losna, Norway. He and his tribe were landowners of some consequence. When Queen Margaret merged the three kingdoms of Norway, Sweden and Denmark, she did not retain the best features of each. At least, my pride of ancestry won't permit me to believe that she did. For the Erlandsons of Losna refused to have anything to do with the merger, retiring, in a collective huff, to the town of Voss and there establishing themselves in the hills. Generations elapsed, the hills remained the same, but it became harder and harder to make a good living.

The traditional venturesomeness of the Norsemen, aided by infiltrations of Irish blood acquired when the earlier and hardier Vikings invaded Ireland looking for trouble and returned to Norway with colleens for wives, breaks out at intervals. With my father it broke out when I was about five. The World's Fair was to be held in Chicago. Dad, by profession a stationary engineer and by avocation a carriage builder, wanted to show his wares at the World's Fair. He went to America. Later, he sent for his family. My mother took her daughters and her only son to New York and we were duly admitted through Castle Garden. My only equipment for life in the new country was a Norwegian vocabulary, a fervent memory of home cooking combined with pleasant recollections of skiing and skating among the Voss Mountains. How my mother ever managed that tedious voyage which I still recall with qualms; how she guided us through the intricacies of entry, knowing nothing of English, and took us into the heart of a new, strange and bewildering country without mishap — how, in brief, she achieved the first step in our Americanization unaided by anybody, is one of the millions of minor miracles that are of the stuff and fabric of America.

Perhaps it was a trick of fate that the first natives of the new country to register favorably with me were not only natives, but aborigines — Indians. In the elysium of the World's Fair, with its glittering palaces, amazing crowds, a towheaded Norwegian youngster was lost one day. Elated by an award of a medal for his exhibit of a carriage, Dad had failed to check my natural curiosity. So I wandered all over that paradise of sights and sounds and smells, having a glorious time on popcorn, pink lemonade and the new and delightful rite of the hot dog. At length — and it must have been a long time — I wound up before a reduced facsimile of an Indian reservation. The contrast between me, a white-haired Nordic fresh from the original source of supply, and the jet-haired Indian papooses, must have struck some minor Indian chief. When the Fairgrounds police, in their nightly hunt for youngsters lost, stolen or strayed, came to item 181-B, specifying a Norwegian boy who knew no English but might respond to the name Knute Kenneth Rockne if pronounced *Kan-ute*, with pressure on the K's, they gave it up. Until morning. Then a weary copper, passing the Indian reservation, beheld a blond head surmounted by feathers, bobbing through a scampering mob of Indian kids, wielding a wooden tomahawk and yelling for scalps.

They promptly collected me, stripped me of Indian finery and restored me to my puzzled parents. Ever since then I've held Indians in affection and esteem, unmodified even by collision on the football field with the greatest Indian athlete of them all. For when, as a professional player for Massillon, Ohio, I undertook the job of tackling Jim Thorpe and learned, while prostrate, following sudden and severe contact, that Mr. Thorpe was no respecter of even all-American persons — the Indian sign became more than an empty phrase.

We'll get back to that. Before I was to see and meet Indians again, a Chicago childhood and youth had to be gone through. It was not unpleasant going. The new, spacious city, with its endless corner lots and tolerant police, was a great place for a boy to grow up in, in the era B.C. — Before Capone. Our baseball and football games were undisturbed by rifle-fire and the popping of pineapples. At that, there was excitement enough for everybody.

We lived in the Logan Square neighborhood — chiefly inhabited by Irish and Swedes. Chicago's broad ethnology called all Scandinavians "Swedes." The Irish were clubby; so were the Swedes. My lot was naturally with the latter. On a huge vacant corner boys of the two nationalities would meet on Wednesday and Saturday afternoons in impromptu and sometimes violent contests. A husky, middle-aged copper named O'Goole kept a paternal eye on us. When the Irish lads were pounding us Swedes, O'Goole strode up and down the sidelines grinning. To onlookers who protested that he should stop the free-for-all, he said, "Nonsense! It's an elegant game, good for the youngsters. Look at Patsy Regan there knock that Swede lad from under a punt."

A few of us, dissatisfied with constant lickings at the hands — and feet — of the Irish, scouted other neighborhoods for bigger Swedes. When bigger boys couldn't be found, we enrolled a couple of bruiser-like Italians on our side.

O'Goole strolled by while a bigger and better battle was in progress and the Irishers were getting a free and liberal taste of mud.

"This won't do at all," he said, striding to the midst of the battle and grabbing Swede boys by their necks. "The game is altogether brutal and unfit for small boys.''

We could only even matters by appealing to the precinct captain to send us a Swede cop as well as O'Goole to supervise our games. Then mayhem was balanced for both sides.

My first real baptism of mire was received in one of these neighborhood corner lot games. I was an end on the Tricky Tigers — historic rivals of the Avondales — so-called because we had a wow of a triple pass behind the line when we wanted to impress opponents and onlookers. Our equipment wasn't elaborate. No helmets, one shinguard per player. We tied our ears with elastic tape to prevent spreading.

Many of us graduated to the Barefoot Athletic Club of older boys, mostly Irish. In a crucial game with the Hamburg Athletic Club for the district championship, trouble came in handfuls. Crowds lined the gridless gridiron and broke into it as the game progressed. Irish sympathizers were militant. Only seven policemen were there to hold back the mob. Things grew more pleasant as the more pugnacious spectators slipped away every now and then for refreshments at nearby saloons.

The game was held in a huge lot opposite the White Sox ballpark. My part in it was not brilliant, but dramatic. In those early days I had spindly legs, which I've retained, and speedy feet, which left me long ago. When the call to carry the ball came, I'd lay back and sprint. That afternoon the call came. Spurting in an end-run with the Hamburg boys after me, my path to a touchdown was clear. Not a Hamburg player was in front. But Hamburg rooters came to the rescue. They threw me and swiped the ball. A minor riot ensued, with players on both teams being pommeled impartially. There were so many players' noses punched that a police sergeant would let only players with noseguards wade into the crowd.

Most of us returned home that evening with evidence of a strenuous afternoon's sport. For me, this was a serious matter. As a football initiate, I played the game surreptitiously, my parents sharing the general belief that football was a system of modified massacre. My most prized possession, a pair of patched moleskin football pants, had to be smuggled in and out of the house. Scars of battle in the Hamburg game betrayed me. My football career was squelched. As it was nearing winter, this didn't matter much, for when spring arrived with the crack of baseballs on bats, I went out with the rest of the sandlot gang. The family approved baseball. During a vicious, extra-inning game with the Maplewood boys, a hot argument developed. Being blessed or bothered by hidden strains of Irish ancestry, I found myself in the thick of it. Suddenly a bat bent on the bridge of my nose. I went home blinded, but uppermost in my mind was not sorrow, but logic. The family had banned football because it was dangerous.

"And I got this nose from baseball" was my triumphant reply.

With full parental approval, when high school days arrived for me, I went out for football, after making the high school track team as a half-miler. There occurred the inspirational picture of Walter Eckersall in action. Likewise, such prodigies of sport as Rube Waddell and Three-Finger Brown took niches in what there was of my mind.

Rube Waddell was a figure to inspire any athletically-minded youngster with the easy glory of games. We knew something of his tradition: how he had jogged on to a crowded ballpark in Harrisburg, driving a team of mules and a wagon, himself attired like a scarecrow; how, after parking mules and wagon by a players' bench, he took possession of the pitcher's box and struck out 12 men in a row.

The Rube always played up to the youngsters. He'd guide droves of us into the ballpark, free, and we'd even follow him miles and miles in his eccentricities. He'd take French leave from his club, go to Libertyville or some other town and pitch for a local semi-pro outfit. The man was a great showman. I remember once in a semi-pro game, he turned dramatically in the box, waved in all the outfielders, sent them to the bench, and struck out every batter.

In those days, I yearned to follow in the footsteps of Waddell, or that other fine pitcher, Three-Finger Brown. That meant having exceedingly sizable feet, which may be one reason why I never became a pitcher, but an outfielder. When the football bug hit me after seeing Eckersall, the diamond's luster dimmed. And the first big thrill of my life came when, at 13 years of age and weighing one 110 pounds, they put me on the scrubs of the North West Division High, now Tuley High in Chicago. In the scrubs we had some slight coaching. Our sandlot football was what the professors call eclectic: we pinched whatever plays we had seen and could remember.

We were keen for signals. Half the fun of the game was the solemnity with which our corner-lot quarterbacks would shout, and we would receive, the long litany of signals. Only colored players excel sandlot boys in love of signals. Two teams of Negro footballers I once umpired for devised a baffling code. Both named their plays after dishes. Pork chops meant a smash through right tackle, pig's feet a run around right end, fried chicken a split buck, and so on. Very confusing to spectators and hardly less confusing to the players. The only worthwhile thing I recall about that strange game is that one side, led by a quarterback yelling items off a menu, marched down the field and paused on the 1-yard line for the team pilot to scream in final challenge, "Now, boys, over that line with the whole blame dining car!"

High school football in those days had all the enthusiasm but none of the finesse of today. Coaches were few. Two professors, Peters and Ellis, volunteered to teach our school squad. They did a good job of it, if only by holding me back and making me realize there was something more to football than the ball. It took me until my senior year to get on the team. Chicago followed our high school games in huge crowds. In those days our team — North West Division — beat the powerful Marshall High, tied with Crane, and bowed only to North Division High, whose second team licked us. The first-string players, led by Wally Steffen, now Carnegie Tech coach, joshed us from the sideline.

Then the name of Amos Alonzo Stagg rose on my horizon. Not in connection with football, although I knew something of his fame. It was a favorite trick of the crowd I played with to hook into the University of Chicago football field through the motorcar gates, guarded less closely than the turnstiles. We saw Eckersall run his team against squads whose names were almost mythically great to us — teams like Northwestern, Haskell and Michigan. My ambition then was to become a quarterback. When Eckersall wasn't on the field, Wally Steffen or Lee Maxwell directed the Chicago plays. Each had a snap to his style that made the quarterback's job the focal point in the football drama. That was right. But a good quarterback needed all of many qualities, only a few of which I had — the principal one being speed.

Coach Stagg supervised an annual series of interscholastic meets around Chicago. The half-mile was my specialty. With the fondness for coincidence that all of us share, many have asked me whether or not Stagg and I met in those days. If we did, it must have been under the stands when I dropped out of longer distance footraces, as invariably occurred. But persistence at track meets won me a small reputation, and when a whimsical switch to pole-vaulting brought me in the news by making an indoor record of 12 feet and 4 inches — which today wouldn't qualify a boy to be a mascot—I began to think I'd arrived.

While in high school, I got on the Chicago A.A. Junior team, after making the grade in one of the numerous athletic clubs dotted around Chicago. In minor meets, the chance to win depended as much on quick wits as stopwatches. Youngsters were quickly initiated into the tricks of the athletic trade. One official timer was known for his distaste for continuous Irish victories. When he was officiating and our teams faced stiff and conquering competition, somebody on our side would always stand near this official and holler of a winning opponent named Schmidt, "Watch that O'Brien come", or of a Thorgensen, "Look at that Reilly jump." But chickens come home to roost. Once when I was bold enough to sub for an absent teammate in an 880 sprint for what I thought was record time, some malicious bird yelled "Come on, Kelly" as I dashed down the lane. The non-Hibernian official overheard: the record was not mine.

The interim between finishing high school and entering college — four years, to be exact, was the principal period of my not-too-celebrated career as a track athlete. I carried the colors of Irving Park A. C. and the Central Y.M.C.A., for which I managed to win the half-mile in 2:20, a good mark then, and graduated to the Illinois Athletic Club. In various meets, I ran against old-time stars like Lindberg, Harvey Blair, Ward and Belot. Martin Delaney and Dad Butler were our coaches, and we newcomers were able to touch shoulders with Olympic stars like Ralph Rose, Lightbody, Hogenson and Irons — and even the great Johnny Hayes, winner of the classic Olympic Marathon over Dorando, came to Chicago to fraternize but not to compete with us — because Johnny had turned pro.

If anybody wonders why it took so long for me to get from high school to college, the answer's easy. I was obliged to earn a living. Football, save as a spectator, was neglected, and I relied on track competition to keep in physical shape.

I had hoped, at high school, to make my way in college. To that end, I learned how to earn more money and save it. A Hebrew boy and I got the summertime job of cleaning our high school's windows at good pay. But other boys, possibly jealous over our appointments, would break windows, invade the school, switch door signs from doors with coarsely diabolical wit and commit other sabotage for which the amateur window-cleaners were blamed. Naturally, we were fired.

But with an urge for the public weal, I took civil service exams for the mail service and received appointment as a mail dispatcher. At this time, I was ambitious to go to the University of Illinois and I set in my mind a goal — to save $1,000 and march on Champaign for an education. Athletic fame was secondary, for, to me, college players loomed as supermen to whose heights I could never aspire.

It seemed more and more likely that any college would have the opportunity to matriculate or reject me as years of night work ensued, my prep school being the sorting room of the post office.

About the most a clerk could earn was $100 a month. He could make his job soft or hard by taking simple or complicated routines. I took the hard routine of dispatcher to have something to do in a temple of loafing. If a clerk took Southern territory, he wouldn't have much to remember because few railroads fed the South from Chicago. But if he took the dispatching job in Illinois or Eastern territory, he had to memorize every main line and branch line train and amend that knowledge with all the timetable changes made by the railroads.

It took me a full year to learn the dispatching scheme or routine. Most of the old-timers called me a fool to tackle a tough job. But there was excellent memory training in it. Even now, I carry a map of Illinois and several Eastern states in my mind and know just what main lines, branch lines and spur lines touch which territories. This has been a good investment in mental energy, and if a football coach needs one thing more than another, it's a memory for the swarming details of plays and combinations of plays — especially the personal styles of coaches and players in executing them. Indeed, it's not the least useful function of a coach's memory to remember what he himself has done that worked or failed in any given emergency.

For the rest, civil service taught me little save its unevenness and unfairness. Going on the job with a zeal to make good and get promoted, you wondered at first why veterans smiled at youthful ardor and industry. I used to hustle letters into pouches just as fast as I could grab them and think of train times. Older hands chatted leisurely as they riffled the mail. The reason for this was that merit meant nothing. The politicians got soft jobs for their favorites regardless of civil service. Enthusiasm could scarcely survive the discovery that a dispatcher who worked hard, eight hours a night, received less than a henchman who did nothing more arduous for eight hours a day than sell stamps from an irremovable seat on a stool.

I was on the way to develop into the smartest shirker of all, having reached a point of lethargy where it took me an hour to distribute as many pieces of mail as in the first enthusiastic days would have taken me only ten minutes. But fortunately, I had garnered my $1,000 by then.

Notre Dame was scarcely a name to me. Football, by that time, had been eclipsed by track and field. Much as I should like to profess being animated by a burning zeal to go out and conquer in the name of pigskin and be acclaimed a mighty player and a coach of massive intellect, the cold, unembellished fact is that a sister of mine was more ambitious for me than I was for myself. She insisted that a college education would mean more to me and the family than anything else. Also, that I'd be able to waste my time to better advantage as a college track athlete than as a part-time wonder of the campus called the Loop. Two friends of mine, Johnny Devine and Johnny Plant, both runners of more than local note, were going to Notre Dame. When we discussed our plans during a Chicago meet, and I told them I was bound for Illinois, they suggested I go along with them to the Indiana school.

"Why," I remember exclaiming, "who ever heard of Notre

Dame? They've never won a football game in their lives."

What swung me to go there was the argument that I could probably get a job, and certainly get by cheaper than at Champaign.

So I went down to South Bend with a suitcase and $1,000. I'd hardly seen more than two trees at one time anywhere, so my first impression was the sylvan beauty of Notre Dame. Father Stephen Theodore Badin, first Catholic priest ordained in the United States, just a century ago received from the United States Government a square mile of territory — 640 acres — for the sum of one dollar. It was the way at that time to encourage people to take up government lands. Later the Fathers of the Holy Cross who founded and brilliantly conducted the university received from individuals such other gifts as amounted in total to nearly 3,000 acres in the early pre-pioneer days when Indiana was a territory and not a state. By industry and intelligence, they made it an ideal site for a university.

The University of Notre Dame, in 1910, when I felt the strangeness of being a lone Norse Protestant — if the word must be used — invader of a Catholic stronghold, comprised six halls in one of which, Brownson dormitory, I was installed. There were 400 undergraduates, physical training was compulsory, and a fellow wasn't thought much of unless he went out to try to make his hall team for football.

Players on the varsity squad were assigned as coaches to the hall squads. I don't know whether that was an advantage or disadvantage, although in my personal case it brought about my first chance for the big team. My own method, since becoming coach, has been to inaugurate interhall league competition and personally watch all the championship games to spot promising material.

Shorty Longman, an end on Michigan's famous Point-A-Minute Team, was Notre Dame's head coach — the first college coach I ever knew. He was a snappy, belligerent figure who affected a shock of hair after the manner of MacCullough, the actor. Indeed, Shorty (rest his soul!) was a pretty good actor, and during my first year at Notre Dame he had me down in his books as a pretty bad actor.

The university gave me a chance to work off my board and room as janitor of the chemical laboratory, cleaning out the slop buckets and doing minor chores. Somebody stole a gallon of experimental wine from the pharmacy laboratory; I was blamed, and ran the risks of expulsion. So my reputation was not glamourous. When, therefore, Joe Collins, a varsity squad man, recommended me for a chance with the big boys, Longman wasn't enthusiastic.

But he gave me the chance. Freshmen were played in those days, and with a small enrollment we needed them. Longman sent me out with the scrubs in a test game with the regulars. He made me fullback. They should have changed my position to drawback. Never on any football field was there so dismal a flop. Trying to spear my first punt I had frozen fingers and the ball rolled everywhere it wasn't wanted.

Longman kept me in that agonizing game. Finally, I tried a punt. Nothing happened. I might have been a statue of a player trying to punt. Nothing was coordinated. I was half paralyzed. A 200-pound tackle smashed into me. My 145 pounds went back for a 15-yard loss.

Longman yanked me out of the scrubs and sent me back from Sorin to Brownson Hall. I was a dud, a washout, not even good enough for the scrubs.

But the fact remained that I could run, and running was important to a football player. Perhaps, I reasoned, if I tried for a job at end, my old spot on the sandlot and high school teams, I'd have better luck. The first step was to get on the varsity track team, which I did. A track letter gave me the prestige to try once more for the football squad.

In the meantime I had sat at the feet of a learned tramp athlete whose name then was Foley, although he had played for many schools under aliases. He was typical of young men who roamed the country, overflowing with college spirit, regardless of the college. His tongue teemed with professional jargon. He knew all the technique and practiced none of it; yet, so glib was he, that it invariably took a shrewd coach half the season to get wise to the fact that this tramp athlete had only one principle in football, which he pithily expressed: "Avoid 'em." He opened my eyes to a state of affairs in college football which has since been reformed — of the journeyman players who'd leave new names behind them wherever they went and live to a ripe old age, from foot to mouth, so to speak, taking loyalty and sometimes talent with them to whichever alma mater would give them the best break.

On the Notre Dame squad in my first year of football were two stars charged with being ringers, George Philbrook and Ralph Dimmick. As a matter of fact, they weren't, but when Notre Dame went to play Michigan, controversy raged, and for a while it looked as if Dimmick would be barred. He saved the day himself when, recognizing a Michigan player who had seen college football experience elsewhere, Dimmick walked up and loudly commiserated with him.

"You've heard the bad news?" he asked. "It's terrible. They've dropped your youngest son from the eighth reader."

Notre Dame never knowingly enrolled a ringer. We played teams whose purity of enrollment was not quite 99 and three-quarters percent. The Indian schools were careless in that respect, several Indian players changing legal names to Indian names as they switched from one Indian school to another. The famous back, Emil Hauser of Haskell became Chief Waseka at Carlisle; another lad I knew named Dietz blossomed into Chief Lone Star and I always called the celebrated back Pete Hauser, Chief Long Time Eat when I met him playing for his third or fourth alma mater — he shone brightly at training table.

Although a growing youngster, I had the advantage of not being too green when I broke into big football company. I was 23 and able to wear a letter sweater without too much intoxication. There were natural hurdles to be jumped in a social sense, for a lone Norwegian, always mistakenly dubbed a Swede, had difficulties among so many Hibernians. These were largely dissipated when, blushing furiously, I was called on to talk at a football rally and having heard somebody call somebody else just a dumb Irishman I had the good fortune to remark, "There's only one thing dumber than a dumb Irishman." Before the bricks could fly, I explained: "A smart Swede."

Notre Dame was struggling to establish itself in football circles. Its schedules were not strong — Ohio Northern, Marquette and Pittsburgh were "big games." Our equipment was poor. In the first game I played — against Ohio Northern — a guard was so severely injured that we had to use up our lone roll of tape. Later, his substitute in the line cracked up, so we had to take tape off the first injured boy to bind up the second one.

Shorty Longman knew much about football, but he talked much more. Our offense was principally a punt and a prayer varied with an occasional line plunge.

Longman's method was that of the old-fashioned oratorical coach. Before a game, he would enter the dressing room dramatically, toss back his shock of black hair and burst into rhetoric.

"Boys," he declaimed, "today is *the* day. The honor of the old school is at stake. Now or never, we must fight the battle of our lives. I don't want any man with a streak of yellow to move from this room. You've all got to be heroes — HEROES — or I never want to see you again. Go out and conquer. It's the crisis of your lives!"

When I heard that for the first time, I was tremendously impressed. The team went out and all but pushed the opposing team — Olivet — over the fence. The next Saturday, as we lay resting in the dressing room, Coach Longman entered.

"Boys," he detonated, "today is *the* day of days. The honor of the old school is at stake. The eyes of the world are on you. Go out and bleed for the old school, and if anybody has a yellow streak let him —"

I sat awe-stricken. Then I saw Dorais and Bergman, two veterans, yawn.

"What do you think of the act today?" asked Bergman.

"Not so good," said Dorais. "I thought he was better last week."

One oration a season is quite enough for any football squad. Action brings reaction, and if the coach talks too much, his words lose weight.

From my first coach, Longman, came another valuable lesson. A sturdy man and useful with his fists, he believed that the best way to impress his charges was to demonstrate that he was physically their master. With this in mind, he prescribed boxing lessons which he himself would give, beginning with the lightweights and working his way through to the heavies of the Philbrook displacement.

Respectfully the squad gathered to see the first demonstration. Several of the less heavy boys, myself included, were to be operated on with boxing gloves. Shorty selected a mild-mannered chap named Matty Matthews, a light end, for the first object lesson. That was a bad break. Matthews stepped out expertly, ducked and weaved and hooked and jabbed. After three minutes Shorty had enough. There were no boxing lessons for the rest of us.

But if Shorty Longman taught me the methods to avoid as a coach, he impressed me with the value of perseverance. Mistaken as may have been his psychology, for boys will never do their best if they are bullied, he none the less pursued his players with a ruthless energy that got results.

Our next coach was Jack Marks, the Dartmouth back. He

made us over from a green, aggressive squad into a slashing, driving outfit. The first time he looked over Eichenlaub — the Notre Dame 200-pound torpedo — Marks showed he knew his stuff.

"We're playing Wabash this afternoon, Eichenlaub," Marks said. "Jones, Feeney and the rest will make the holes. You tear through them."

"But I'm only a poor high school boy," said Eichenlaub.

Marks turned on his heel. That afternoon, Eichenlaub ripped through Wabash for total gains of more than 400 yards. The Wabash squad piled on a streetcar for the depot, badly licked. The car stopped for an old lady carrying parcels. She worked her way through the limping Wabash players while a wag cried, "One side! Here comes Eichenlaub's mother."

Marks was always a quiet mentor, but he liked to pile up scores. Once we led Adrian by 71 to nothing, and the Adrian coach said he'd used up all his substitutes and would we agree to let him send men back who had already played. Marks agreed. He returned to the sideline. Some time later he saw a strange player on our bench.

"You're on the wrong bench," he said.

"I know it," said the lad. "I've been in that scrap four times already and they're not going to send me back if I can help it. I've had enough."

Marks laughed quietly, and let the lad remain. Again, during a game with Butler, a big halfback named Meyers — strong but shy — was missing.

"You've only got ten men on the field," the umpire cried to the Notre Dame coach.

Marks looked over the field in anger. "Where in heck is Meyers?" he demanded.

"Here I am coach," sang Meyers from his blanket. "I got bumped right on my knee."

Marks smiled quietly, said nothing. But Meyers played no

more. That was his method. The team stepped out under his leadership so that gradually we came to be noticed a little beyond the Midwest. I won a regular berth as end under Marks and had the pleasant surprise of seeing myself discussed as an all-America possibility toward the end of the 1912 season. Almost imperceptibly it seemed to me, I was established in football. One year, practically abandoning the idea of continuing the game; the next, being talked of — never mind by whom — as an all-America prospect.

Then the end of football and college career impended. Father died, and it seemed imperative that I quit school, although it's on the record that I passed my special subject, chemistry, cum laude. A wise sister interposed.

"If you quit," she said, "all right. You may earn a living, but it will be as a mail dispatcher."

So I went back, and I had scarcely got off the train at South Bend when I was greeted by a cordial voice.

"You're Rockne?" he said.

"Well," he went on, after having introduced himself as Jess Harper, Notre Dame's new coach. "I'm grabbing you football men off the trains as fast as I can. We've got to work our heads and legs off."

"What's the excitement?" I said, trying to be calm.

"They're letting us play in the East," he exclaimed. "The Army has agreed to play Notre Dame."

COLLEGE DAYS AT NOTRE DAME

Take the number of football players of the past two generations, multiply by five or six — and you'll have an approximation of the countless thousands who have thrilled to some lad's participation in his first big game. So we'll save time by assuming it is understood that Alexander trampling the Persians, Napoleon smashing the Austrians at Jena, and One-Eye Connolly crashing the gate at Toledo are faint, carbon copy thrills to the beat and jump of a young man's pulse when he is sent on the gridiron for his first big-league performance.

Mine came in the game against Pittsburgh in 1911. Notre Dame had played four games that season before meeting Pittsburgh. Our record was 182 points against 6 by our opponents. True, the opposition was not strong — although Ohio Northern and Butler, two on the list of four, were never exactly pushovers. Really, my debut was against Ohio Northern. An almost disastrous debut. Charlie "Gus" Dorais, our quarterback, threw a forward pass at me, but I was so high-strung and tense that I met the ball with frozen fingers and dropped it — and at the same time learned that loose hands and relaxed fingers are the only effective tools for making the soft, non-resisting catch essential to a forward pass receiver.

Against Pittsburgh we were rather cocky. The Panthers were a powerful outfit under Coach Duff. They had beaten some of the best in the East. But we had been so used to piling up points that when the first quarter ended with only zeros on the scoreboard, the experience was so novel it flustered us.

What seemed like a big crowd watched the game — about 10,000 — and the local press had spoken much, perhaps too much, about the brains and speed of Dorais, our steersman.

Dorais, a 140-pounder, had both; but Pittsburgh had its quota. To break the scoreless tie after the first half we tried desperately to show the cagey Panthers that we could outguess them. We did, catching them napping with an onside kick by Dorais which I scooped up and raced to make a touchdown. But the officials outguessed us, and decreed no score and a penalty of 5 yards against Notre Dame.

To offset this disappointment and to give the crowd another sample of the tricks in the Notre Dame bag, Dorais — always a quick thinker — decided to drop called signals. The plan was to play our right and left halfbacks, Al Berger and Dutch Bergman, without further notice, depending upon which side, right or left, Pittsburgh aimed its punts.

This was new and smart stuff. Wagner, Pittsburgh's 190-pound ace, kicked a long ball to Bergman's side. After the runback and first down we went into scrimmage. Dorais called no signals. But our center, a big husky chap who, up till then, had been eminently satisfactory, failed to snap the ball back.

Precious seconds passed and our chance for a surprise play was lost. Officials cautioned us to hurry; Dorais prodded the center, linemen yelled at him.

"All right," he barked back. "What's the signal?"

Dorais calmly called one of our routine plays, and the game went on. In the huddle he berated the defaulting center, reminding him how it had been agreed to have a surprise play around end without signals.

"Next time you plan a trick," the center said, "don't whisper it. I'm half deaf."

Failure to discover that fact before the game cost us a chance to score against the great Panther team. But Wagner's play had something to do with it. He was a big, strong, speedy man, and he seemed to have made it his life's work that afternoon to stop the even speedier Dorais. Anybody who saw him play will agree that Dorais had the best open-field legs in football. The news lads, who were digging into dictionaries for labels at that time, called Dorais the Will-o'-the-Wisp. Usually, he was, but not against Mr. Wagner.

We had developed a new and effective way to cut down interference. It was to race behind the man and instead of flying low with arms and hands for a tackle, to hurl the body at his heels. He'd fall like a ton of brick and stay where he fell. It also had the advantage of hurting nobody very much, and gave onlookers a dramatic touch. Several Pittsburgh players tried to copy this cut-out against Dorais. He was too fast.

Like all small fast men it was impossible to tackle Dorais in the orthodox way of diving at his legs. But Wagner, an all-America player, had all-America brains. Instead of diving at Dorais' legs, he ran at him and threw his arms around his neck, stopping him dead. If I had to curb Mr. Albie Booth's enthusiasm in a match against Notre Dame, that's how it would be done. It's the only way to stop the nimble-footed speed kings.

That evening a disappointed bunch left Pittsburgh after a scoreless tie; but I had learned three things in that initiation into "big league" football. Most important was the high Wagner tackle; second was the fact that when you catch your opponents napping and put over a fast one — as with the onside kick that should have won the game — officials may also be napping and call offside what was onside; third — that a large crowd meant no thrill to me. Overawed by what looked like assembled millions as we ran on the field for the kickoff, the moment the ball went into play I had promptly forgotten that anybody was looking on. It was all a valuable part of football education.

Puzzling to me was not only that we were disappointed, but that the crowd, as interpreted by the sportswriters, felt that we had failed to pull off any miracles of forward passing, the new and then little-understood aerial game.

There has been so much guessing and dispute as to where this aerial game originated, and so many have thought that Notre Dame held and holds the patent, that a little research should settle the question. As with most revolutionary movements in established practice, the forward pass came in quietly, almost obscurely. Eddie Cochems, coach at St. Louis University circa 1907, enrolled a few boys with hands like steam shovels who could toss a football just as easily and almost as far as they could throw a baseball. St. Louis played, and defeated, several big teams — using the forward pass. One would have thought that so effective a play would be instantly copied and become the vogue. The East, however, had not learned much or cared much about Midwest and Western football: indeed, the East scarcely realized that football existed beyond the Alleghenies. Old-fashioned line plunges, mass plays and the monotonous kicking game waiting for a break were the stock in trade. The pass was a threat which heavy teams disdained. Warner of Carlisle and Stagg of Chicago were just behind Cochems in evolving the open game.

In all, with the pass as a versatile weapon, there are only about 90 possible plays on attack. Since a football team is no stronger than its weakest player, the number of practicable plays mastered by a team is rarely more than 20. The pass complicated matters too much for old-fashioned technicians, who preferred to rely upon bull strength and Lady Luck. This accounts for the slowness of its general adoption.

We took it up the instant we saw it. Dorais — the name, by the way, is pronounced like the first two notes of the tonic sol-fa scale — and I spent a whole summer vacation at Cedar Point on Lake Erie. We worked our way as restaurant checkers and what-not, but played our way on the beach with a football, practicing forward passing. There was nothing much else for two young fellows without much pocket money to do, and it made us familiar with the innovation that was to change the entire character of football.

Jack Marks, our coach, had tried a quarterback to end pass combination in several games. Against Wabash in 1911, our first year with the pass in full play, Wabash had us beaten on a long and perfectly executed pass from Lambert to Howard. But the officials measured it. It was thrown more than 20 yards beyond the line of scrimmage and therefore illegal. Wabash was penalized. Also, had that pass been thrown within five yards on either side of center there would have been another penalty. If you can figure out the sense of those rules, you're much better than I.

In football, technically, there are three kinds of forward passes. First, the spot pass, thrown to a spot where the receiver is supposed to be; second, the pass which is thrown to one definite individual; third, the choice pass in which the passer, dropping back for protection, selects whichever of his eligible receivers is uncovered. This is the best pass in football, but the most difficult to execute.

About the time of which I'm speaking, Wabash had a clever exponent of the choice pass named Skeets Lambert. He was responsible for an extra restriction eventually being put on the forward pass by the Rules Committee. For instance, when we played Wabash we would rush Lambert and chase him sometimes 20 to 25 yards beyond the line of scrimmage, and it looked as if we were about to throw him for a big loss. However, he fooled us by purposely grounding the ball when there was no teammate uncovered to whom he could pass. The ball was returned to the spot at which the play had started, with loss of down but not of yardage. Dorais promptly borrowed this trick from Lambert. In turn, Pritchard of Army copied it from Dorais, but Pritchard got credit as a gridiron fox for this quarterback ruse, which a subsequent rule penalized. Many football tricks of offense and defense have had similar genealogy — the player who performs them before the most newspaper witnesses being usually credited as the originator.

Perfection of the forward pass came to us only through daily tedious practice. I'd run along the beach and Dorais would throw, from all angles. People who didn't know we were two college seniors making painstaking preparations for our final football season probably thought we were crazy. Once a bearded old gentleman took off his shoes to join in the fun, seizing the ball and kicking it merrily, with bare feet, too, until a friendly keeper came along to take him back where he belonged.

But the fruit of our summer work was evidenced in the fall. In the first three games before meeting the Army for the initial game of a now historic series, Notre Dame piled up 169 points to its opponents' 7, South Dakota being the scoring foe. This was all done on forward passing. Although we were not the first to use the forward pass, it can be truthfully said that we were one of the first to learn how it should be used.

In the early days, the players threw it and caught it much like a medicine ball. A football weights 14 ounces and a medicine ball about 14 pounds. When you catch the latter it's in a hugging grab. We mastered the technique of catching the football with hands relaxed and tried to master the more difficult feat of catching it with one hand.

Naturally, we had pointed all this aerial practice for the Army game. The West Point boys were the background for Notre Dame's first big Eastern appearance, and while the game was not all-important to them, to us it was the supreme test of our playing careers. The Army had a marvelous line, with two all-America stars, McEwen at center and Merrilot at end, while Pritchard at quarterback also shared all-America rating.

The morning we left for West Point the entire student body of the university got up long before breakfast to see us to the day coach that carried the squad to Buffalo — a dreary, all-day trip. From Buffalo we enjoyed the luxury of sleeping car accommodation — regulars in lowers, substitutes in uppers. There was no pampering in those days. We wanted none of it. We went out to play the Army like crusaders, believing that we represented not only our own school, but the whole, aspiring Middle West.

West Point, as always since our meetings have become famous, treated us most hospitably. We were housed in Cullum Hall and given the freedom of the Officer's Club. There was a fair crowd to see the game on the Plains, and the New York newspapers were interested enough to send second-string football reporters. The Cadet body and most of the other spectators seemed to regard the engagement as a quiet, friendly workout for Army.

For the first part of the first quarter it looked that way. An Army line outweighing ours by about 15 pounds to the man, pushed us all over the place before we overcame the tingling realization that we were actually playing the Army. I recall Merrilot shouting, "Lets's lick these Hoosiers!"

So I asked him, in a lull, if he knew how the word Hoosier originated.

"We started it at South Bend," I informed him, John Markoe and what other of the Army team would listen. "After every game the coach goes over the field, picks up what he finds and asks his team, 'Whose ear is this?' Hence, Hoosier!"

The gag didn't work so well. Something else did. After we had stood terrific pounding by the Army line, and a trio of backs that charged in like locomotives, we held them on downs. Dorais, in a huddle, said, "Let's open up." It was amusing to see the Army boys huddle after a first, snappy 11-yard pass had been completed for a first down. Their guards and tackles went tumbling into us to stop line bucks and plunges. Instead, Dorais stepped neatly back and flipped the ball to an uncovered end or halfback. This we did twice in a march up the field, gaining three first downs in almost as many minutes.

Our attack had been well-rehearsed. After one fierce scrimmage I emerged limping as if hurt. On the next three plays, Dorais threw three successful passes in a row to Joe Pliska, our right halfback, for short gains. On each of these three plays I limped down the field acting as if the thing farthest from my mind was to receive a forward pass. After the third play, the Army halfback covering me figured I wasn't worth watching. Even as a decoy he figured I was harmless.

Finally, Dorais called my number, meaning that he was to throw a long forward pass to me as I ran down the field and out toward the sidelines. I started limping down the field and the Army halfback covering me almost yawned in my face he was so bored. Suddenly, I put on full speed and left him standing there flatfooted. I raced across the Army goal line as Dorais whipped the ball and the grandstands roared at the completion of a 40-yard pass. Everybody seemed astonished. There had been no hurdling, no tackling, no plunging, no crushing of fiber and sinew. Just a long distance touchdown by rapid transit.

At the moment when I touched the ball life for me was complete.

We proceeded to make it more than complete. The Army resisted. They charged with devastating power and drove through us for two touchdowns, with the score at halftime being Notre Dame 14, Army 13. In the second half Army changed its defense to meet our open game. It didn't work. Dorais, always alert, reversed our tactics sufficiently to take over the Army line-plunging game with Ray Eichenlaub as our spearhead. He ripped the Army line to pieces.

In the last quarter, Army closed up to stop Eichenlaub. Dorais instantly switched tactics, opening up with a fresh barrage of passes that completely baffled the cadets.

Fitzgerald, a guard, took special interest in McEwen, Army's great center. Their contest grew personal as Army lost ground and we gained it. Superheated between scrimmages, wild words flew. Fitzgerald closed in on McEwen. He socked McEwen square on the jaw, then instantly yelled as he did so, "Hey, referee!"

The referee turned around just in time to see McEwen crash home a right to Fitzgerald's nose. McEwen was promptly ordered from the game, but as captain of our team I had to stop and explain that both boys had been too boisterous and so the referee let both of them stay in the game. From then on their decorum was more proper.

Hard-fought to the end, this first Army game, with its score of 35 to 13 in favor of Notre Dame, does not quite represent the difference in playing quality between the two teams. The Army was much better than the score showed. It was, however, the first signal triumph of the new, open game over the old, battering ram Army game. And the Army was quick to learn. Press and football public hailed this new game, and Notre Dame received credit as the originator of a style of play that we had simply systematized. Our achievement was that we had demonstrated, by completing 14 out of 17 passes in this game against the Army, gaining some 200 yards thereby, that the forward pass was an integral part of offense and not merely a threat. Recognizing this, Army later in the year went out itself and forward passed to victory by 20 to 9 over one of the strongest of Navy teams.

Looking back over that match and its surprising revelation to Army players versed and skilled in the old-style game, it's no wonder that they could not solve the forward pass problem in a single hour. Indeed, after 20 years of making and directing forward pass attack, I know of only one genuinely effective way of stopping it, besides the obvious precaution of covering the five eligible receivers — the ends and backs — and that is to rush the passer: a tactic at once crude and unrefinable.

Another new thing the Army learned was the Notre Dame experiment in boxing tackle. George Philbrook, the gigantic Notre Dame tackle, who weighed 220 pounds, gave me very good reason to be resourceful when I was a scrub and he was a regular. Philbrook had terrific hands. He made my life miserable until I practiced for hours the head bob and shoulder drop that Young Griffo, the fighter, used so successfully in the ring. It was a feint followed by instantly applied power and it worked. With this as a starting point I devised the Notre Dame style of "boxing" a tackle. Other systems invariably used two men to block the big boys. By employing the smarter strategy of feinting with head and shoulders, we have made it practicable for one man to block one man, no matter what the discrepancy in weight.

No varsity team was ever acclaimed as the crowd of us that returned by Pullman to Buffalo and by day coach from Buffalo to South Bend.

When we got off the sleeper at Buffalo we were surprised at the cordial manner in which station employees received us. One man we gratefully remembered. He said, "Football team?"

We agreed we were.

He said, "Breakfast's ready," and led us to a corner of the station restaurant where an elegant meal was served.

We had just finished the repast when in walked a big squad of athletes — who were exceedingly outspoken when they found their meal had been devoured. They were the Syracuse football team en route back home from a game with Michigan — the breakfast spread was intended for them!

At South Bend, the whole town turned out. Brass bands, red fire, speeches; as if we had repulsed and conquered an attack upon the West by the East. What particularly impressed everybody was the fresh appearance of the squad. A grueling game with Army was supposed to punish those on the receiving end so that they showed signs of wear and tear for weeks. We didn't find the Army so rough at all. Hard-hitting, clean and fair then, as they have been ever since.

In all my experience as a player the toughest game I ever survived — apart from a professional game in which Jim Thorpe participated and nearly parted me in two — was the Notre Dame-Texas game on Thanksgiving Day 1913. The temperature in Austin was 86°, while we had left Chicago freezing. It nearly ruined us, but the Texan boys seemed to like it. Halfback Simmons is generally remembered as the terror of that team because of the astonishing and dangerous dive he made over the heads of would-be tacklers. Nobody else has ever done anything like it. He'd run rapidly with the ball after receiving it from center and dive head first regardless of what, where, or when he might hit. It ended in a complete somersault — unless somebody got him, which was not often. (In that case he was lucky not to break his back.)

Mr. Simmons, if he reads this, will learn that he caused me no end of trouble — and the Notre Dame players a grand laugh. Our team was dog-tired. Feeney, Dorais and the others stood about the field like wilted statues. I myself was on the verge of collapse. Finally, I grew so tired that when Simmons started on one end run I faded out, stopping dead. Simmons cut back and ran right into me. I hung on to him and as I got up, I looked around and saw that not a single man on our secondary defense had moved an inch to help me. They all burst into an ironic cheer.

"Attaboy, Rock!"

What I thought need not be printed here.

But Mr. Simmons' somersaulting hurdle was solved in the second half. As he came thundering at Joe Pliska, Joe crouched, lifting his shoulders at the moment of impact, and just as Simmons went to dive, Eichenlaub, our fullback and Al Feeney, our roving center, hit him. He was carried from the game which we all regretted. Simmons was a great back without his foolish diving which only left him open to injury.

A giant hunchback tackle had been treating me rough when he was sent in as a sub toward the end of the first half. He left me with a limp so that in the rest between halves I dreaded returning, getting myself set mentally, for 30 minutes of hell!

I've played against many strong linemen, but never against one as strong. This man was a murderer. In that — to us — terrific heat, he smashed into me like a ton of animated ice. I was glad when the half ended. I might mention in passing, that in the dressing room a strange newspaper man regaled us with the tale of a Texan — a spectator, not a player — who saved a game once by actually shooting down a dropkick before it could cross the bar.

I was happy when my friend — who apparently belonged to the wrong social set and so was not played as a regular — was not in the lineup in the second half.

Fate was with us. A cool northerner, as they call them in Austin, blew up between halves, and we went out for the second half with the temperature comfortably reduced. Opening up with passes, we scored two touchdowns. Everything was rosy. Another touchdown for us and the game seemed in the bag, with only 10 minutes to go. But the Texas coach returned the hunchback to the line, and the hunchback returned to me. He knocked my poor, sweating, ill-treated carcass sideways, backways and allways. Suddenly, I had an idea. Elward, my substitute at end, was just 10 minutes short of the 60 minutes' big-game play necessary to win a football monogram, emblem of team membership.

I called to the coach, "Send Elward in — he needs ten minutes for his monogram."

"Darned nice of you," said the coach as I hurried out of the game."

"If that hunchback does to Elward what he's done to me, he won't think I'm so nice!"

If this seems to confirm a once prevalent impression that Western football was legalized rioting, that's far from the truth. Moguls of the game in the East seemed to think the football boundaries were limited by the Alleghenies on the west, the Berkshires on the north and the Philadelphia City Hall on the south — if not yet stolen. Likewise they thought the principal, indeed, the only inhabitants of this kingdom of football were the Big Three — Yale, Harvard and Princeton — with Penn and possibly Cornell and Dartmouth as neophytes in the sacred circle. Only when Western teams had the audacity to invade the East and beat Eastern teams did football consciousness expand nationally.

There were scores of fine players in the West, and great games every week that received little but local publicity. Only when a Western team fought a big Eastern school did it stand a chance of headlines. Later, with the football public converted to the idea that while East is East and West is West, the twain had met somewhat to the advantage of the West, a new sensation in football, such as Willie Heston, Eckersall, the Praying Colonels of Centre College or the Galloping Ghost, Red Grange, could be front-paged and made famous overnight. I could name a dozen players who — had they the opportunity to do their stuff against schools with better-known names but certainly with no better brand of football than the schools they played — would have been as celebrated as long-remembered stars.

Acquisition of fame stimulates individual and organization. Nationwide discussion of Notre Dame by football followers after the first Army game had a tremendous effect on our own varsity spirit. Everybody in the school, save the older professors, wanted to be a football player. I recall even Cy Williams, celebrated home run slugger of the Phillie Nationals, clamoring for football togs. As he came out on the field for first practice he said, "Come on, fellows, let's kick up a few flies." The baseball coach barred Cy from football, afraid that Cy might get hurt.

This inspirational drive, resulting from recognition in the East, marked all Notre Dame's players. I know of only two instances where it didn't. Once against Penn State, Pliska, a fine player otherwise, had an off moment. A Penn State end went clattering by him while Pliska stood rooted to the ground, staring into the grandstand. The end caught a forward pass and scored.

We ragged Pliska in the dressing room, and he took it. He had to. Later he confided to me, "I was wondering about a girl in the grandstand. I heard her holler, 'Attaboy, Joe!' I looked for her and missed that end going by."

An expensive distraction for us, but excusable. Certainly more so than another case when the surge of college spirit missed its mark. And a colossal mark. His name was Frank Milbauer, and hundreds of players who bumped into him will remember him painfully as Notre Dame's 180-pound tackle. Milbauer was a huge eater. Ordinary players would consider a hot dog a snack. Milbauer wanted nothing less than a porterhouse.

In a game our B team had with De Paul in Chicago, he was sent in at a critical moment when the ball was on our 1-yard line, with about 30 seconds to go, and a large crowd of De Paul rooters hysterical with excitement. Just as signals were called by the De Paul quarterback for the final play, Milbauer said to the guard next him, "I hope they've got a big dinner tonight. I'm gettin' kind of hungry."

The play smashed through him for a score. No wonder.

Winning of our spurs had a heady effect; but at Notre Dame they had a pretty good tradition for what they called "knocking down the ears" of conceited players or students. Coach and professors supplied the balance between achievement and self-esteem when the ordinary vicissitudes of the game failed to do so. In my own case, when I felt cockiest, at a time that the Midwest papers spoke glowingly of my chances to be named on the All-Western team, I heard that an impressive crowd of football writers had gathered to see Notre Dame play Marquette in Milwaukee. This seemed an opening to show them they were not far wrong in talking my name for All-Western honors. It happened to be a kicking game.

Quarterback Huegel of Marquette caught a long punt, and I chose the play to show my stuff. Laying my ears back I tore down the field to tackle him, putting on all the speed I had to impress the newspaper boys. Of course, on approaching the ball carrier I should have slowed down and spread my feet for the tackle. I didn't. I kept running fast. The ball carrier just sidestepped and I went flying by — feeling foolish.

Humility is the lesson every football player, indeed, every athlete, must learn in secret commune with his soul or he gets it in big doses on the field of contest with thousands to witness. I recall being very cocky at an intercollegiate track meet between Purdue, Indiana and Notre Dame. I'd won the broad jump — 22 feet, 6 inches, and placed second in the pole vault with a 12-foot hoist and also second in the shot put — making 11 points, the highest individual score of the day. Chestily I went into the discus throw, without any real reason, as I was not and am not a discus-thrower.

After the event the announcer bawled results. So-and-so 130 feet, another so-and-so, 120 feet — then, in a roar that I thought could be heard in South Bend, "Rockne of Notre Dame — 76 feet, 8 inches."

Instantly I perpetrated the only alibi of which I've been guilty. I limped from the field clutching my right arm — the throwing arm — as if it had been crippled.

Conceit of any kind is a handicap to an athlete. My own experience on the gridiron convinced me of this. And I've seen plenty of confirmation in the conduct of others. One of the most uppish lads I remember made the carrying of information from coach to team on the field an occasion to dramatize himself.

Now information on football varies a lot, depending on whether you get it from a coach, player, student, alumnus, newspaper man or whether you are one of these lucky chaps who get it direct from the barber himself.

This particular player made his biggest bid for fame when we were playing Pittsburgh. With five minutes to go, the score nothing to nothing, our coach became rather irascible with the quarterback and turned around to the bench to a third-string quarterback with instructions to go in there and open up. The poor little chap went out there with his knees knocking because the only thing he had ever opened up in his life was an umbrella. Taking the coach literally, on his own 20-yard line with 80 yards to go, he called for a very complicated play, a double pass followed by a long, backward lateral pass. We tried the play and the double pass was all right but the long, backward lateral pass found no one to receive it and the ball rolled along and finally stopped on the 1-yard line where it was pounced upon by Lindsay, the Pittsburgh left end. As we lined up on defense it looked as though it was all over but the shouting, because it didn't seem as though we could possibly hold Pittsburgh who now had the ball on our 1-yard line with first down. When it all seemed darkest there was suddenly a ray of sunshine through the clouds because tripping from the bench gamboling along came our hero — a frolicking sub-guard who was replacing Turk Oaas, our regular left guard.

Now the rules state very clearly that no substitute coming in may speak to his teammates until one play has elapsed. And so as he lined up with us he said nothing actually but he looked out of a beaming countenance as though to say, "I carry vital information from the coach." Immediately our morale came right up. We said to ourselves: If we can only hold this team for one down the afternoon may yet be saved because this lad is carrying the mystic formula from the coach himself. So on the next play all of us charged so low and so hard that as we picked ourselves off the ground one by one there was the ball, still 1 yard from our goal line.

Enthusiastically and with our ears up like a lot of donkeys we turned to the sub and asked breathlessly, "What did the coach say? What did the coach say?"

We took time out as the new sub paced back 5 yards to make sure the other team wouldn't hear. Then he said, pompously, "Boys, the coach says to hold 'em."

Although I had been in a score of matches, my own mother had not seen me play the game until I felt quite sure she would not be disappointed in her son. This was, perhaps, a touch of vanity, but no boy wants his mother to see him try anything athletic unless or until he thinks he's pretty good at it.

So as captain of the team I brought my mother down from Chicago to see me play. It was a comparatively easy game for us, and I had plenty of openings to make individual plays — long runs and so on. All of which I did. When the game was over — we had beaten our opponents by about 60 to nothing, I sought out Mother. She was pleased to the point of enthusiasm, but not with me.

"That player," she said, "Isn't he wonderful? I mean the one who does the pinwheels."

He was the cheerleader.

There were others, too, who did not think football the be-all and end-all of existence. Discovery of at least one of these, a person of great importance to us of the Notre Dame football squad, was surprising — almost suppressing.

At training table the football players were given fine food and plenty, but forbidden to eat pastry. Nonetheless, pies were served to stimulate strength of will in abstaining from them. Non-players, knowing that the pies were present and would not be used, invaded the training table room to steal the pies. Objecting to this intrusion we'd beat them off with a barrage of buns.

Especially luscious pies — strawberry pies — were served one day and thrust aside. Envious eyes lighted on them, and hungry hands reached out. The bun barrage was violent, and at its highest moment the door opened and there entered a dignified gentleman in black who received a bun squarely in the right eye from me. He was President Cavanaugh of the university.

Instantly he demanded that the football squad be disbanded and the football schedule for that season canceled. Here was a resolute gentleman who had been prominently connected with the affairs of Notre Dame for about 30 years, and it looked as if it were curtains for football there.

We formed an impromptu committee to explain matters to the prexy. He was very kind.

"I couldn't reconcile," he said, tapping a damaged eye gently, "men like you who are good in your classes, with ruffians who throw only footballs and buns."

We made more explanations. They must have satisfied. Football remained and, later, it was the same President Cavanaugh who appointed me head coach.

But in the retrospect of my playing career, one hard day stands out above all others — the day I tried to stop the greatest football player of all, the Indian, Jim Thorpe.

My job was to tackle Thorpe, which I did, successfully and with much suffering, three times. After the third time Thorpe smiled genially at me.

"Be good boy," he said. "Let Jim run."

He took the ball again and I went at him. Never before have I received such a shock. It was as if a locomotive had hit me and been followed by a 10-ton truck rambling over the remains. I lay on the field of battle while Thorpe pounded out a 40-yard run for a touchdown.

He came back, helped me to my feet, patted me fraternally on the back and, smiling broadly, said, "That's a good boy, Knute. You let Jim run."

78

THE FOUR HORSEMEN

A sleepy-eyed lad who looked as though he were built to be a tester in an alarm clock factory, loafed about the backfield in the Notre Dame freshman lineup for practice. With him in the backfield, his companion halfback, was a youngster who appeared to be half-puzzled by everything going on. Between them was a smaller and wirier boy with a sharp handsome face and a clear commanding voice. These assets seemed the best the youngster had, for in his first plays during that practice game he made as many mistakes as he called signals — and he called a lot. As a rule, rookie quarterbacks do.

It was not an inspiring practice to watch. Even the likely-looking youngster at fullback, who could run like a streak, ran quite as often into the hands of tackles as through slits in the line. After watching this backfield performance for an entire quarter, I shook my head.

"Not so hot," I thought — especially when the entire four were smeared by a clumsy but willing scrub tackle who weighed about as much as the entire quartet and pounded through like an ice wagon to block a kick.

"Not so hot," I repeated preparing to exercise the virtue of patience and wait another year for a sensation like George Gipp.

This freshman bunch could be whipped into a combination of average players. Not much more.

That was all the dream I had of them that day. And it didn't come true.

Three years later, this trio with another took the field to the cheers of 50,000 people at the Polo Grounds and dazzled into defeat the strongest Army eleven ever sent against anybody. The next morning Grantland Rice rose to lyric heights in celebrating their speed, rhythm and precision, winding up a litany of hallelujahs by proclaiming them "the Four Horsemen." Whereupon an enterprising young gentleman in South Bend perched the returned victors of the backfield on four borrowed nags and sold the resultant photograph to the tune of a small fortune.

These accidents will happen in the best of all possible worlds. Indeed, the football epic of the Four Horsemen is the story of an accident. How it came to pass that four young men so eminently qualified by temperament, physique and instinctive pacing to complement one another perfectly and thus produce the best coordinated and most picturesque backfield in the recent history of football — how that came about is one of the inscrutable achievements of coincidence of which I know nothing save that it's a rather satisfying mouthful of words.

Harry Stuhldreher, the quarterback, hailed from Massillon, Ohio; Don Miller, halfback, came from Defiance, Ohio. Jimmy Crowley, the other halfback, hailed from Green Bay, Wisconsin; and Elmer Layden, the dashing, slashing fullback had his home in Davenport, Iowa. The four did not play as backfield in their freshman year — remember, I had seen them in practice and survived the experience unimpressed.

These men and the others of the freshman squad in 1921 were soundly beaten by such teams as Lake Forest Academy and the Michigan State freshmen. Stuhldreher, of the lot, had the most promise. He sounded like a leader on the field. He was a good

KNUTE ROCKNE — Knute Rockne, head football coach at the University of Notre Dame from 1918 to 1930, directed his Fighting Irish to 105 victories in 13 seasons. He is considered by many to be the greatest, and certainly the most charismatic, college football coach of all time.

THE ROCKNE FAMILY — Lars and Martha Rockne raised four daughters and a son, Knute (standing at right).

ROCKNE THE TRACK STAR — *Although football became his life's work, Rockne's accomplishments as a varsity athlete included middle-distance running and pole-vaulting.*

WINNER AS A PLAYER, TOO — Rockne played end on the 1913 team that upset the Army 35–13. During Rockne's playing career at Notre Dame, the team won 24, lost 1 and tied 3.

AS AN ACTRESS? — Rockne cut a splendid figure as an "actress" in a school play.

THE GIPPER — The legendary George Gipp starred for Notre Dame before a tragic illness ended his life in 1920, less than two weeks after he had been named an all-American. In 1928, Knute Rockne asked a discouraged Notre Dame team to beat the Army and thereby win one for the Gipper. A legend was born.

A FILM TRIBUTE — In 1940, Warner Bros. released KNUTE ROCKNE — ALL AMERICAN, *a film biography of the Notre Dame coach. Actor Pat O'Brien gave a memorable performance as Rockne. The role of George Gipp was played by a young actor, Ronald Reagan, in his most famous role. Forty years later, when Reagan became President of the United States, his most popular nickname would be "the Gipper."*

WORLD PREMIERE — The Colfax Theater in South Bend, Indiana, hosted the world premiere of KNUTE ROCKNE — ALL AMERICAN, a motion picture starring Pat O'Brien in the title role, on October 4, 1940.

THE FOUR HORSEMEN OF NOTRE DAME — The famous words of sportswriter Grantland Rice: "Outlined against a blue-gray October sky the Four Horsemen rode again. In dramatic lore they are known as famine, pestilence, destruction and death. These are only aliases. Their real names are: Stuhldreher, Miller, Crowley and Layden. They formed the crest of the South Bend cyclone before which another fighting Army team was swept over the precipice at the Polo Grounds this afternoon as 55,000 spectators peered down upon the bewildering panorama spread out upon the green plain below."

FATHER — *Rockne was a good father who loved his four children, Billy, Jackie, Knute Jr., and Mary Jean. He is shown with Jackie and Mary Jean.*

MR. AND MRS. KNUTE ROCKNE — *Knute met his wife, Bonnie Gwendolyn Skiles from Sandusky, Ohio, while working at Cedar Point during the summer of 1913. He married her on July 15, 1914.*

KNUTE AND HIS BOYS — *Rockne poses with his sons, Billy, Jackie and Knute Jr.*

TEACHING BABE THE BASICS — *Rockne starts with the basics while showing baseball star Babe Ruth a few of the finer points of football.*

TWO VERY FAMOUS MUGS — Knute Rockne mugs for a photo with his good friend, Will Rogers. Upon learning of Rockne's sudden and tragic death in a plane crash, Rogers, the great American humorist, was heard to say in sadness, "It takes a big calamity to shock this country all at once, but Knute, you did it. You died one of our national heroes. Notre Dame was your address, but every gridiron in America was your home."

AT THE OFFICE — Although he was one of the most famous men in America, Rockne maintained a humble office. Here, he is shown answering correspondence with his secretary, Ruth Faulkner.

AN UNFORGETTABLE VOICE — *It was said that in the 1920s, there were three unmistakable voices in America: crooner Rudy Vallee's, humorist Will Roger's, and Rockne's. Rockne raspy, staccato style captured audiences wherever he spoke.*

and fearless blocker and as he gained in football knowledge he showed signs of smartness in emergencies. Layden had speed — he could run a hundred yards flat in less than 10 seconds at a track meet. But speed and some kicking ability seemed to be all his football wares. Jimmy Crowley was only less humorous in play than in appearance. He looked dull and always resembled a lad about to get out of or into bed. He showed very little as a freshman — certainly none of the nimble wit that made him as celebrated for repartee as for broken-field running. Don Miller traveled, that first year, on the reputation and recommendation of his brother, "Red" Miller, the great Notre Dame halfback who made such havoc when his team beat Michigan in 1909. Red had sung the praises of another Miller, Jerry, who made a fine high school record, but couldn't add to his poundage of one hundred and thirty-five and, unfortunately, grew quite deaf, and so was disqualified for the tough going of big-league football. Don, who also ran in his freshman year, surprised me when he came out for spring practice and with his fleetness and daring sized up as a halfback to cheer the heart of any coach.

In the fall of 1922, Notre Dame had lost all its veteran backs except Paul Castner at fullback and Frank Thomas at quarterback — one of those decimations by graduation that give coaches gray hair or, as in my case, remove what little hair they have.

This 1922 squad, the first on which the Four Horsemen got their chance, romped through its preliminary games against Kalamazoo, St. Louis, Purdue and De Pauw. With the first big game looming, against Georgia Tech, Stuhldreher was promoted to alternate as quarterback with Thomas, Crowley and Layden were assigned to alternate as left halfbacks, while Castner, the veteran, remained at fullback and Don Miller received the right halfback berth. Crowley won his place only by a surprising performance against Purdue, when the sleepy one astonished Purdue a great deal and me a great deal more with the liveliest exhibition of cutting, jumping, sidestepping, change of pace and determined ball-toting that I had seen in many a day.

The Georgia Tech game of 1922 found the Four Horsemen ready to demonstrate. The experienced Castner guided them through their green patches, but practice had displayed their unusual gift for synchronization. They showed it against Georgia Tech, for the first time and were largely instrumental in turning in a 13 to 3 victory.

Yet in that same game, Stuhldreher, who had appeared most promising of the bunch, made the biggest mistake of his career — one that stamped him still an apprentice quarterback. When our team reached the 5-yard line Stuhldreher passed on second down over the goal line for a touchback, and it became Tech's ball on our 20-yard line. Never again did Stuhldreher make a tactical error while running the team as quarterback. That statement goes unqualified. I have in mind the uproar that followed his spectacular, or what seemed to be a spectacular, error during the Tournament of Roses game against Stanford on New Year's Day in 1925. Notre Dame was ahead, yet Stuhldreher passed straight into the hands of a Stanford player. The fact is that Stuhldreher had hurt his foot, badly. We didn't know until the game was over that he had broken a bone and was suffering agony throughout the game. Even this circumstance, of course, could not excuse passing on second down with his team leading.

But Ed Hunsinger, our right end, had told Stuhldreher in a huddle that the Stanford halfback who should be covering him, Hunsinger, did not follow him deep into the scoring zone on Notre Dame's offensive plays. Knowing this, Stuhldreher opened up on second down and called for a forward pass from himself to Hunsinger. Sure enough, on the play, Hunsinger got clear away from the Stanford halfback, who failed to follow him deep enough. He was clear in the open, ready to race for a touchdown on receipt of the ball. A 45-yard pass would have done the trick, and a 45-yard pass straight to the target was easy enough for Stuhldreher. But not this time. As the plucky little quarterback squared himself to shoot, bringing down the foot with the broken bone to make his stance, excruciating pain shot through him, so that instead of his usual vigorous throw the ball sailed a feeble 20 yards.

Yet Stuhldreher's tactics were sound — for so good a ball-thrower. For even if Hunsinger had failed to catch the ball and it had been intercepted, a 45-yard pass would have been as useful as a punt. If Hunsinger had caught it, it was a sure touchdown. The worst thing that could have happened would have been an incompleted pass, which would have cost us a down. As the play took place on third down an incompleted pass would not have hurt because Layden was there to kick the ball on the next play. And Layden was a kicker!

It is good to be able to set down this inside story of what many thousands may today regard as Stuhldreher's "bone," ranking it with Merkle's failure to touch second and Riegel's celebrated reverse-English run.

Stuhldreher was really a master of sound quarterback play. He could read through another team's strategy without a key to the code. Against Army in 1924, Stuhldreher found their ends were smashing in close, with the result that he sent Crowley and Miller circling the ends. In the very next game, against Princeton, he found the tackle and end on each side were very wide, so he confined his tactics all day to sharp thrusts by Layden through the thinned-out line, and cut-backs by Crowley and Miller. In the game following that, against Georgia Tech, he made gains back to our weak side, because Georgia Tech had shifted over to our strong side, thus leaving the weak side unguarded. And in the game against Wisconsin, fairly strong that year, Stuhldreher repeatedly found a gap between tackle and end that netted neat gains. To prove conclusively his versatility, when Nebraska's line in the next game was exceedingly tough before a fast-plowing backfield, Stuhldreher wasted little time or strength on line drives. He opened up a passing attack and completed ten before the final whistle, the score being 34 to 7.

This diversity of attack caused a well-known football writer to wonder what the Four Horsemen could do with a kicking game. As if in direct response they put one on in their last appearance for Notre Dame in that Tournament of Roses game against Stanford. The entire team had wilted in the heat. The boys were unable to move. They had to rely on Layden's punting, not their usual game. Layden, however, got off a pair of punts around 80 yards which were quite useful. Stanford lost the game despite its hard smashing play, and Pop Warner was disappointed, making much of the fact that Stanford had made more first downs than Notre Dame.

To this comment, Crowley, as spontaneous spokesman for the Four Horsemen, pointed out that the score was 27 to 10, adding, "Next year in the major leagues they aren't going to count runs that come over the plate. They'll just count the men left on bases." Pop Warner, like the grand old sport he is, admitted Crowley had the laugh and that the only payoff in football was the ball over the line and not down close to it.

Crowley was always quick at a comeback. After one big Eastern game an official who had penalized Notre Dame all afternoon to the neglect of the Eastern team, which he rarely looked at, met Crowley, and they trudged side by side into the dressing room.

The official said to Crowley, "You were lucky to win today."

"Yes, Cyclops," said Crowley. "After watching you officiate you don't even begin to know how lucky we were."

Crowley was the gagman of the outfit, but not at first. You never saw a more serious bunch of football players than the Four Horsemen before they had really made good, or a gayer group afterward.

One afternoon Crowley came from vacation into my office. This was after fame had perched on his sloping shoulders.

"Ran into a grand high school player in Green Bay, Coach," he said.

"Good, is he?" I asked.

"Awful good," he said.

"You really mean that, Jim?" I said.

"He's awful good," said Crowley.

"You mean — as good as you?" I asked.

"Well," said Jim, edging toward the door. "Perhaps not that — but awful good."

He vanished.

The official debut of Crowley and the other Horsemen as big leaguers was actually against Carnegie Tech in 1922. Castner, the veteran fullback who had been their bellwether in the early games, was so seriously injured in the game against Butler — a broken hip in a flying fall — that he was out for the season. That does not often happen with Notre Dame men and I've always regretted its happening to brave old Castner.

I moved Layden from left halfback, where he had been alternating with Crowley, to fullback. These boys surprised the football fans of Pittsburgh with their perfect timing as they functioned for the first time as a unit backfield. Layden amazed me by his terrific speed as fullback. He adopted a straight-line drive that made him one of the most unusual fullbacks in football. He pierced a line through sheer speed — cutting it like a knife, although each man in the opposing line outweighed him by twenty pounds. His power was not wasted in plunging! Compared with the orthodox fullback, he was like a saber compared with a club.

They won. This victory, however, didn't thrill me as much as the defeat they suffered the very next game — against Nebraska. The Cornhuskers had one of the heaviest teams in their history

— and they are known for very active heft. They pushed the relatively little Four Horsemen team all over the field. At the half the score was 14 to nothing, and it would have been another touchdown if the lightweight boys from South Bend hadn't held the Nebraska heavies on their 1-yard line for four straight downs. They emerged from the battering a sadly crumpled team.

But they came out fighting mad for the second half, whacked across a touchdown in the third quarter, and carried the ball to Nebraska's 1-yard line toward the end of the final period. Stuhldreher called for a pass, and Layden spurted ahead to a corner of the field where he was all set to receive and down the ball for six more points. But Stuhldreher, the alert, this time was not alert enough. Weller, the huge, 250-pound Nebraska tackle, crashed through the line and smeared the 150-pound Notre Dame quarterback.

Our college alumni in Lincoln had a banquet ready for the Four Horsemen team that night. But Crowley, who came through the drumming bruised and bandaged, put it this way, "We need a thermometer more than a feed."

They went to bed to nurse their sore spots.

In the lobby of the hotel after that terrific game — which made me prouder than ever of the Four Horsemen because it proved up to the hilt that they could stand punishment of the hardest kind — Monte Munn, old Nebraska tackle, since renowned as a man-mountain prizefighter, bawled frequently at me, "I told you so!" A trifle piqued I walked over to find out what he meant. To my surprise I learned that it had been the practice of an enterprising young man of unknown name and address to print rush orders of postcards with my photo on them and beneath it the score of the Notre Dame-Nebraska game plus the legend: *I told you so.* These he sold like hot cakes to our rooters, for Nebraska was a hot rival and we had won the three previous years.

This was my first realization that anybody achieving a faint measure of celebrity could be exploited without his consent. The Four Horsemen had a similar experience, and so did a young footballer named Red Grange.

The Four Horsemen once were blamed for a breach of football etiquette in which they were in no way involved. This was against Wisconsin in 1924. We had the game well in hand, so in the second half the Horsemen were taken out and sent to the showers. In the final two minutes of play a substitute Notre Dame halfback went in for Crowley and strutted his stuff by running for a touchdown. As he crossed the line for the score he thumbed his nose at a Wisconsin player pursuing him. He was instantly yanked from the game. Many thought Crowley had made the vulgar gesture — but that was never Crowley's idea of wit.

His style of thought and good-humored balance of character were of the sterling stuff that wears better in adversity than in success. Against Princeton he and his three playmates were at their best. But Crowley faltered once. He had taken the ball, skirted Princeton's shock troops, and begun one of the rhythmic runs of the Four Horsemen. Slagle of Princeton ripped up the field to meet him. Crowley veered and Slagle nailed him from behind. The Four Horsemen did not look their customary efficient selves at this sudden full stop to their progress.

In the dressing room between halves sleepy-eyed Jim Crowley was apologetic.

"I made a mistake," he said. "I didn't know Slagle was that fast. I should have cut back."

"That wasn't the mistake you made," I said. "That wasn't it."

"Yes, it was," he said. "I admit it. A mistake."

"No," I said. "Slagle didn't know who you were. If you had shown him those New York clippings you've been saving, telling how good you were, he wouldn't have dared come near you."

Crowley laughed louder than anybody else at this. Perhaps he knew, what all the team knew, that the Four Horsemen — great though they were — received a measure of praise that they should have shared with the stalwart linemen — whom we called the Seven Mules.

This caused a few timely prods from some of the Mules. Adam Walsh, our center — a tower of strength for the Horsemen to play behind — watched them try unsuccessfully to get started on one of their famous runs against Lombard, with a second-string line to screen them. There was nothing doing, so I shot in Walsh and the other six Mules.

"What seems to be the matter, boys?" asked Walsh, as he took the ball to snap back for the first scrimmage. "It seems you need a little help."

This banter helped to check the rising tide of self-esteem which only the rarest of young athletes can stem in face of wholesale flattery. One of the Horsemen suffered just a trifle from swelled head. It was cured in short order. This particular Horseman stalked into the squad manager and asked for a clean pair of stockings and a new belt.

The manager said, "O.K., but turn in your old ones."

"What for?" said the Horseman.

Rip Miller, one of the Seven Mules, standing within earshot among five of the other six, rebuked the manager, "What do you mean?" he said. "Talking that way. Don't you know who this is? This is one of the Four Horsemen."

"No-o?" said the manager, in mock awe.

"Ye-es," said Rip, in more mock awe.

As the Horseman walked away, confused, manager and players stood staring, while the players nudged one another, murmuring reverently, "He's one of the Four Horsemen."

The lad was cured. Next morning he went forthwith to the manager and said his old stockings and belt would do.

Those Horsemen were pretty good themselves at concerted kidding. Against Army in 1924 they had been warned in practice of the prowess of Garbisch, the great Army, all-America center. When they met him he punctuated some of their attempts to get away. They found a neat way to irritate Garbisch. On subsequent plays, when the drive was against him, and he was smeared, one Horseman would politely inquire of another so that Garbisch, picking himself up from the ground, could overhear, "Is that the great Mr. Garbisch?"

To which another would solemnly reply, "Yes, that's the great Mr. Garbisch."

When on another smash the all-America center was floored, Crowley would ask of Miller in amazement, "You don't mean to say that's the great Mr. Garbisch."

And Miller would retort, "If the number's correct it's none other than Mr. Garbisch in person."

It didn't help Garbisch's game much.

Quick to block and banter opponents, the Horsemen, through their most articulate member, did not spare themselves when they failed. I tried to make Jimmy Crowley a triple-threat man. He could pass and run in great shape, but his kicking was good for just about 40 yards. This was, perhaps, due to an unusual fault. He would take three steps with the ball — and that made his kicking dangerous as he held the ball too long and there was risk of the defense breaking through and blocking it. He practiced for weeks to kick almost simultaneously with receipt of the ball. So, when Layden became slightly injured in the Princeton game, Crowley was assigned to do the punting. On the first try, his old bad habit returned subconsciously and he took three steps. A fast-charging Princeton tackle broke through and blocked the kick, which rolled over our goal line for a safety and two points for the Tigers.

After the game was over a teammate chided Crowley, "I see you're a triple-threat man, this year."

"Yes," snapped Crowley. "Trip, stumble or fumble."

While this joshing on the part of their squad-mates lasted, the Horsemen took the best means to offset it by joining in the chorus. On the only day in a great season that they weren't able to shine — against Northwestern at Soldier Field, Chicago, they expected razzing. Northwestern was an inspired team, while the Four Horsemen were off-key, off-color, stale and plainly unable to get anywhere. We won from Northwestern but only after a heart-catching, nip-and-tuck game.

On the train returning to South Bend, a gentleman who had gazed upon the rye when it was golden, barged into the car containing the squad. The conductor requested his ticket. The drunk brushed him aside.

"Where are you going?" the conductor demanded. "New York, Toledo or Cleveland?"

"I don't know," sighed the inebriate. "I guess I'm not going anywhere."

Jimmy Crowley turned to his teammates and remarked, "Must be one of the Four Horsemen."

This self-recognition of their weak moments was part of their almost irresistible strength when working in smooth mechanical order.

Layden, a quiet member of the quartet, was their star on defense. His ability to intercept passes was uncanny, and it never had more value than in our Tournament of Roses game with Stanford on New Year's Day 1925. Pop Warner — greatest originator of smart plays — had a forward pass play that enabled him to win a tie for the Pacific Coast Championship even without the help of Nevers, his all-America fullback, who had been injured most of the season. Nevers was in the lineup against us — and what a game he played! Twice after Stanford had advanced to about our 30-yard line they called for this dangerous pass out into the flat zone, and both times Layden, jumping high in the air, tipped and caught the ball and ran for touchdowns.

This provoked Crowley to remark after the game was over that the best play Notre Dame had was that pass from Nevers to Layden. Pop Warner's sage comment was, "It's a great play — either we score or our opponents score!"

Each of these Horsemen shone individually on his day. As Layden's was against Stanford, so Miller's was against Princeton. Miller was the most dangerous of the quartet at right half, once in the open field. His long runs for touchdowns were a feature during his three years of play. But he was a much better defensive player than he has been given credit for being.

In this Princeton game in 1923 Miller had just gone off right tackle for what looked like a good gain when he fumbled the ball which went rolling along the ground. Quick as a flash, a Princeton back, trained in the alert Bill Roper way of stooping at full speed and picking up a loose ball, scooped it up. The next thing we saw was this Princeton halfback with two interferers in front, speeding down the field. The goal line was 75 yards away — and no one between the runners and that goal line but Don Miller.

Wasting no time after his "bone," Miller had recovered poise and was racing across field to cut off the Princeton men. The stands were in an uproar. It seemed impossible that Miller could overtake them, or, if he could, be of any resistance against three men.

Watching this swift-moving drama, I figured that Miller might do one of three things. He might make a wild effort to rush the two interferers or get at the ball carrier. In that case, failure meant a sure touchdown. He might have tried to sidestep the two interferers by clever footwork and dodging. Again, that meant time, and failure meant a sure touchdown. He discarded these two obvious bits of strategy. He did the third thing.

Pressing his speed he ran in front and to one side of the two interferers, crowding them toward the sideline. He feinted in and out to slow up the Princeton cavalcade, and did this so calculatingly that by the time they were within 20 yards or so of the Notre Dame goal line our fastest end, Clem Crowe, had had time to rush up and tackle the ball carrier from behind. The touchdown was not scored, and so Miller redeemed his fumble by as heady a piece of work, and as well-executed as any I have ever seen.

Crowley, the sleepy-looking wit, was the nerviest back I've known. He would throw himself anywhere. Also, since I'm using superlatives, where they belong, he was the greatest interferer for his weight I have ever seen, and a particularly effective ball carrier on the critical third down.

Examine their record closely, and you'll find the Four Horsemen stand unique as a continuing combination in the backfield. They lost but two games out of 30 — both of these to the heavier Nebraska team — in 1922 and 1923. In the 1923 game their speed was seriously handicapped by the condition of the field. Nebraska had just built a new stadium, and had been unable to grow grass on the gridiron. The clay field was hard-baked, so, to prevent unnecessary bruises to the players, this field had been plowed to make it soft. A well-meant procedure, but it applied four-wheel brakes to the Horsemen.

But these lads of the colorful cavalry of Notre Dame need no alibi. The record's good enough. And the same is true of their scholastic records. They retain their interest in football while attaining success in business. All are coaching the game. Stuhldreher, the quarterback, coaches Villanova University; Don Miller, the Navy line; Jimmy Crowley, Michigan State; and Layden, between spells at the practice of law in Pittsburgh, coaches Duquesne University. While Adam Walsh, leader of the Seven Mules that bore the brunt for the charge of the light brigade of the Four Horsemen, is an engineer and coaches the Yale line.

This quartet of backs, destined to be immortal in football, caused me labor, sometimes caused me pain, but mostly brought great joy, not only to their coach but to the spectators. Only their fame was a bit embarrassing. At their heyday I was hounded by newsmen and sob sisters trying to get collective and individual interviews, genealogies and prophecies with, by and for them. One determined lady pursued them for pieces to appear in an obscure journal — by mail, telegraph, telephone and on foot. Finally, she caught up with Crowley.

"Who on Earth is she?" he was asked.

"Oh," he said blandly. "She's the third horsewoman."

And Biblical students of the Apocalypse will recall that the third horseman personified pestilence.

An accident of Blasco Ibanez' best-selling popularity inspired their name; by accident they were brought together. But it was no accident that made them collectively and individually fine players. That was design and hard work. The Four Horsemen have the right to ride with the gridiron great.

BUILDING A WINNER

The first time I ran on a gridiron as a varsity player against Ohio Northern, a one-man welcoming committee made himself heard. He had far less grace but much more voice than my friend Grover Whalen. He uttered one stentorian yell, "Who's the homely Swede at end?"

Roars of laughter greeted this sally. I was disconcerted. It was like being hit with a missile. Although fairly thick-skinned under criticism, this personal slap in public carried a sting.

It had its influence in helping to formulate one of my first principles in coaching practice: never to ridicule a beginner. You can kill talent before it starts by a smart crack at the wrong time.

The football coach's greatest asset is his greatest responsibility: the reliance placed upon him by the boys in his charge. I regard the handling of personnel as the most important part of the coaching job, and whatever secret of success there is to it can be reduced to a simple formula: strict discipline in training and on the field of play combined with kindly interest in all other relations with the boys.

A very good player named Charlie Bachman gave me my first test of authority when I was an assistant to Jess Harper. Bachman was being put through blocking practice. Someone evidently gave Bachman what he considered better advice than mine. I worked with him for half an hour one afternoon only to see him discard the blocking method I had taught him — a quick, spread step and low crouch. There was only one thing to do. I did it.

"Come out of there, Bachman," I called. He came out. "Go to the showers and turn in your suit. We won't need you any more."

There was consternation at an assistant coach firing a varsity squad man. But Harper sustained me. Later, Bachman explained that somebody had told him Rockne might be a good, all-America end, but his knowledge of blocking was limited. Bachman apologized, was returned to the squad and played with credit in many big games.

This example gave me the reputation of being a martinet — a reputation valuable to any coach provided he doesn't work too hard to keep it.

Let me say at once that Notre Dame scholastic discipline creates the right atmosphere for a coach. There is no coeducation; by far the majority of the 3,000 students live in halls and dormitories on the campus. All but seniors are obliged to eat their meals in the school refectories. Strict hours are kept; class attendance requirements are stern. This latter I know, to my sorrow, for several fine football players have been suspended in my time. It's bad business for a coach to appeal to the faculty in behalf of an inadequate student. I did this once. The boy was given a chance and reinstated. He went into an important game and fumbled us to defeat, illustrating a general rule that a careless student is a careless player.

From the beginning of my coaching career, with whatever faults I brought to my profession, I at least had intelligence enough to recognize that the faculty must run the institution. The school is their school, and the coach must bear in mind that his is an extra-curricular activity like glee clubs, debating societies, campus politics, publications and so forth. Sometimes a coach may be handicapped by the passion in human nature for prerogative and authority which, on occasion, leads the faculty to interfere. But meddling is never the policy of top-notchers. They're too busy perfecting themselves in their own work. If a player flunks in class, he's no good to the coach or the school, and the coach who goes around trying to fix it for athletes to be scholastically eligible, when mentally they're not, is a plain, everyday fool.

The first premise to start with in coaching is that the school wants a good team (and so, of course, do the ever vocal alumni) and the boys want to make a good team. No boy who puts on a football suit and goes out to try for the varsity lacks manliness. Indeed, courage is the commonest quality among football material.

In my early days as coach, we tried an impressive trick that was later discarded. More than 100 boys would race onto the field in football uniforms before a game to give a picture of Notre Dame's reserve strength. This used to surprise smaller squads so much that one smart coach once said to his boys about to leave the dressing room, "Keep your eyes on the ground till you line up."

While it was true that many of the players in our impressive army never got into the game, it seemed to serve the purpose of accustoming beginners to the roar of the crowd, although it had a less desirable effect in spreading the legend that Notre Dame was first and last a football school. This it has never been and never will be. Many schools are richer in material than Notre Dame, which observes all Western Conference rules as to eligibility, training, practice and the rest.

Some 300 recruits step out every March for spring practice. Every boy who wants to try out is given a suit. For the first week we have a little informal competition in which every boy takes part. This competition includes sprinting, tackling the dummy, throwing a ball, catching a thrown ball while running at full speed, kicking a ball, bucking the charging sled, carrying the ball through a live tackler — all of which gives us a pretty good lineup on who's who for the coming season.

The 40 men who look best and who will include the best of the previous fall's freshmen, are picked out and called the varsity squad. These men immediately begin learning the Notre Dame offense. The remaining 260 boys — for no one is cut off the squad although he may drop out if he wishes, are divided into five other teams, which we call Southern Methodist, Pittsburgh, Carnegie Tech, Navy and Southern California.

An assistant coach or a senior who is graduating, teaches each of these squads, from the scouting notes of the preceding season, the offense of these teams which we are to meet in the fall. After a week, the varsity team practices its offense by scrimmaging against the other five scrub teams, and then going on defense they learn how to meet these five distinct offenses as they are interpreted by the five scrub organizations. After three weeks of this, the two men from each of these scrub teams, who make the best showing, are promoted to the varsity squad. This stimulates interest and ambition. That is the gist of our spring training.

Everybody who follows football knows that the game, as played today, is better and less bruising now that brains count more heavily than brawn. As physical and mental training, football is unexcelled for boys strong enough to play it and patient enough to learn it, and I've observed that, aside from those unusual players who have a superb instinct for the game — the players who become great stars — a poor prospect can develop into a good player through application and industry.

Especially, since psychology plays a large part in modern football, can the boy with only an average gift in physique and mentality aspire to and attain his niche in football if he gets careful painstaking instruction, and follows it equally carefully and painstakingly.

Very often during a successful Notre Dame season, the comment is made, even by experts, that the Notre Dame system is mysteriously efficient, a method that has something of magic in it. Sometimes I wish that were true. My job would be much easier. The fundamental fact is that the school is alive with school spirit. Where you have an indifferent faculty and a listless student body, you'll have failure on the athletic field.

Once we played a conference team — an important team. The poor chaps seemed lifeless and were badly beaten. Perhaps the reason was that the students who should have been cheering them on were pursuing their own branch of athletics — mezzanine hurdling at a *thé dansant* instead of supporting their schoolmates on the gridiron.

When more than 2,000 youngsters turn out at bleak gray dawn to give the Notre Dame team a send-off for an away-from-home game, and the same multitude sacrifices sleep and comfort to receive them on their return, you have indomitable spirit behind you.

In 1925, when Army gave us a terrible trouncing, due to the demoralizing effect of a touchdown by Light Horse Harry Wilson in the first three minutes, the student body had seen us off. When we returned, thoroughly defeated by 27 to nothing, not only the student body in its entirety, but hundreds of South Benders welcomed the team home as if it had scored its greatest triumph.

Even the janitors out at the school receive and display the contagion of animated interest. An old walrus-whiskered fellow named Adolphus, supervising steam heat in one of the halls, never failed to have two-bits on the varsity in every game. When we won he bought five cigars and smoked them amid wreaths of smiles. When we lost he consoled himself and annoyed everybody else with alibis.

Returning from a defeat at the hands of Iowa in 1921, the

boys made much of a little curtain lecture I'd delivered to them, the purport of which was that in an evenly-balanced game (score 10 to 7) the other team's better mental poise had beaten us.

Old Adolphus got the returns downtown and went back home in a huff. The next day, Sunday, instead of going downtown as was his wont, Adolphus stayed at home and when the team returned from Iowa City about 2:30 in the afternoon, there standing at the head of the steps of Sorin Hall, waiting to meet them, was old Adolphus, irate.

"What was the matter with you boys, anyhow?" was his first question, in broad Hungarian dialect. "Who lost this game out to Iowa City?"

And Harry Mehre, center, later the coach at the University of Georgia and quite a wag, replied, "Old mental poise lost the game."

Replied Adolphus, in disgust, "That guy never could play, anyhow."

A boy entering Notre Dame from prep school finds himself at once part of an organism complete in itself, a wholly masculine democracy animated by a single spirit. There is, of course, no compulsion to play football, although quite naturally it is insisted for the sake of health and character that the boy take part in some branch of athletics. It does not seem to be generally known that in sports other than football — track and basketball and baseball — the school has an enviable record.

If the newcomer decides to come out for football he realizes at the beginning that he must make his mark in the face of much competition. There are five or six men fighting for each place on the varsity team, and about twice that number contesting for each place on the freshman team or on a hall team.

As typical, take the case of Frank Carideo, all-America quarterback. He's generally regarded as one of the smartest field pilots in the game. When he came to South Bend from Mount Vernon, New York, his high school reputation was good, but in his first appearances with the scrubs there seemed nothing to warrant the prophecy that within three years he'd become the country's outstanding player for his position.

To start, Carideo had — as a mere novice — the three things I regard as essential in a quarterback: a good resonant voice to call signals with authority, a cool alert head and a dominating personality. This is the kind of quarterback who inspires confidence and respect.

Carideo, with other aspirants for the jobs of field general, is given a thorough drilling by the coaches. He has a few flaws — principally being too conservative in his choice of plays. These are corrected. He may be occupied for an entire afternoon, or two afternoons running, doing nothing but passing the ball back to a ball carrier until deftness of motion becomes automatic. Finally, he is picked to go in with a scrub freshman team for a practice game against the regulars.

He doesn't know that a test has been devised — as it always is devised for promising players. The center on his side is a veteran, and in my confidence.

Carideo, aspiring quarterback, goes in to run the second scrub eleven. He's told that he's boss on the field — absolute boss, warned that the coach will watch every play, and only intervene when he makes a glaring mistake. He doesn't know that it has already been arranged for him to make a few glaring mistakes.

Play begins. Carideo's team receives the kickoff, which is brought back to the 15-yard line. The logical thing to do is to punt. Probably Carideo has this in mind. But the Mephistopheles center suggests a running play. Carideo falls for it and calls for the run. Our archconspirator, the center, makes a pass from center so bad that it can't be caught — and, of course, it's fumbled. No need to tell Carideo after the scrimmage that he was in the danger zone where with the conditions as they were, the thing for him to do was to get out of there quickly and safely by punting.

A little bit later one of Carideo's halfbacks is tackled near the sideline. Carideo's next play should be to take the ball out of bounds or run it back into the center of the field. But the veteran Iago, playing center, suggests the punt. Carideo calls for a punt. The center passes the ball over to one side toward the sideline, so that the kicker is lucky to catch the ball at all, and the bad pass having pulled him out of position facing in the wrong direction, the kicked ball can't help going out of bounds almost immediately. No need for me to tell Carideo that he should never punt when close to the sideline. That phrase would have meant nothing to him, but with the experience of this mistake seared into his soul, rest assured he will never repeat it.

Remember, all the time this is going on I am acting as timekeeper of the game, and so I can lengthen or shorten the period as I wish. In this particular scrimmage Carideo's team scored early in the first period and then threatened a score near the end of the same period. They reached the 5-yard line. Carideo then calls for a play and our ever-ready center turns around and calls, "Check." Carideo repeats the play. The center comes back and argues with Carideo regarding his choice of play, giving his reasons why the play shouldn't be called. They line up again. Carideo calls for another play. Center turns around and says, "No, no, Frank." Then he goes back and whispers to Carideo, "Shoot the play right over me and we'll go all the way for a touchdown." The play doesn't gain an inch — or at most, about a yard. Again, Carideo calls signals. Again the same heckling delay and advice by the center. In the midst of this I shoot off the gun announcing the end of the half — Carideo's chance for a score having been lost through indecision and unnecessary delay when seconds were mighty precious. Between halves Carideo asks me, "What would you do under the same situation?" I privately and to one side tell him, because I never criticize my quarterback in front of his teammates and the public. You can't do this and build up confidence in the boy himself or confidence of the players in the boy. What will Carideo do the next time a similar situation occurs? He will tell the center to mind his own business, listen to the play, pass the ball and get his number 12 shoes out of the way so they won't interfere with the ball carrier. He will also keep in touch with time left to play so he can hustle his plays as quickly as possible.

In the next game, where our center and Carideo are still working on the same organization, we allow Carideo to make just two mistakes purposely. The first time he gets down to the goal line our veteran center will suggest a forward pass on first down. Carideo calls for the forward pass, and if it goes over the goal line for a touchback for the opponents, great! He has made one of the most common errors a quarterback can make, and one which he will never repeat.

The second mistake we purposely make is to have him wait till fourth down to kick when deep in his own territory. Again, the center makes a bad pass, the kicker is unable to get the ball. Result: opponents get the ball next to Carideo's goal line. No need for me to discuss these mistakes with Carideo. They are self-evident. We now have the working basis for quarterback play and the center, who, by his timely misplays and bad suggestions has helped to educate Carideo, now retires from the scene, with the satisfaction that he hasn't done such a bad job of education. As a matter of fact, Carideo will visit me in my home some evening and go over with me these mistakes which we purposely had him make. He does most of the talking. I then give him a little theory, which he takes in spoonful homeopathic doses, as it were, so as to make sure that every drop is fully assimilated. I could tell him a vast amount of football just then, but he would only get mental indigestion.

I now give him the four basic principles of quarterback play, which, with the other lessons he's learned, lead him toward the secret byways through the maze of field generalship.

When in doubt, punt!

Know when *not* to forward pass.

Remember what plays are working and what plays are not working — particularly the former.

Look up and see who makes the tackles. It may suggest a play to you.

One or two more practice games and then Carideo is ready to study the strategy map — ready to learn 58 don'ts and 62 do's for a quarterback. He begins to develop his powers of observation so he can recognize a defense when he sees it. He begins to get a sense of values and personnel, both as regards offensive players and defense. He studies when to hustle play and when to slow it up. He reasons when to gamble and when to play safe. He begins to use plays in logical sequence, one play being used to make the succeeding play good. He learns how to pick out a weak spot and avoid strong parts of the defense. He learns when to use Loose-Hipped Harry, who either gains 20 yards or loses 5; when to use One-Yard Elmer, who never gains much but always is good for a yard; when to use Plugging Pete, who never gains much, but whose off-tackle drive is generally good for 3 yards. And, as he develops, all through experiences and a kindly word of advice now and then, he begins to map out plans of campaign against certain teams and certain defenses, always trying to outguess them, never wasting any energy and saving up for the goal line and special scoring plays he has carried all the time under cover in his vest pocket.

That is the development of a quarterback, and we try to train every player on the team to think along the same lines, so that every player can play smart football defensively.

That, elementally, is the system of trial and error. I don't know of any other that can be successful in the intensive training necessitated by the short football practice season.

If it is asked, as it probably will be, whether or not a keen-eyed coach can pick a player of character at first glance, the answer is that a coach with such keen sight would be more of a marvel than any player. The only man who can pick men by taking a look at them is a night clerk, who's suspicious by nature of men without baggage.

Savoldi, who was so popular on the Notre Dame team that the Chicago newspapers referred to him as "the people's choice," is a native of Italy. A sturdy muscular chap, I confess to having had doubts as to his gameness. I confided this to Tim Moynihan and told him to test Savoldi in scrimmage aginst the scrubs. Moynihan relished the assignment. At the first opportunity, he walloped Savoldi — under cover, of course. On the next play, Savoldi ripped through at Moynihan again and took another wallop for his pains. A third play and Moynihan once more cracked him. This time Savoldi knew it was no accident.

Turning to his quarterback, Savoldi said, "Just keep calling for me to carry the ball through Moynihan — he can't stop me."

And the way that terrible Tuscan tore through Moynihan for gains of 5 to 10 yards was an eye-opener for everybody.

After the scrimmage, Moynihan said to me, "Don't you worry about that boy's courage. He can take it and he likes it. And what he'll do to these other teams this fall is going to be just too bad."

Every player is taught how to protect himself in the system I follow. A raw recruit will receive tiresome drill in self-protection during scrimmage. He will be taught to bob his head to avoid slaps and be kept bobbing it for ten minutes at a time; he will be taken to the tackling machines and put through a routine for half an hour at a time at an exercise that teaches him the correct torso position for charging and blocking. His footwork will receive particular attention — how to spread and grip the ground for impact both before and after a run, how to apply the charging power of hips and thighs. He will receive painstaking instruction in the correct stance for his position and how it varies as the play varies.

All the varied attitudes on offense and defense that a player must assume to save energy and induce speed and strength, are reduced to the toil of slow motion. So that the practice field at times gives the appearance of a crowd of eccentric classical dancers taking their time over the next rhythm. All movements are executed simply and individually for a relatively long time until they are thoroughly mastered. Then they are combined and performed simultaneously so at the end of six weeks, by repetition, repetition and still more repetition, movement becomes automatic.

I have often been asked why I start a whole second team and then some time, generally at the end of the first quarter, I insert 11 new men — the varsity. In a terrific schedule like Notre Dame's, I am continually faced with the problem of saving regulars. The second team acts very much in the capacity of shock absorbers. We know by experience that two football teams generally hit the hardest in the first quarter. With a light backfield, like the Four Horsemen particularly, why not save them from this bruising and unnecessary thumping? The second reason is psychological. The varsity, sitting on the sidelines and watching the second string play, become keyed up unconsciously. The third reason is to enable the varsity quarterback to look over the defense carefully and decide his plan of attack.

This, however, is incidental. The main reason is to save them as much as possible from Saturday to Saturday, for boys will be boys — and often they must be guarded against their own zeal for play.

One particular sophomore I recall, was much too eager for the fray. He could scarcely be blamed. His sweetheart was watching the game. He came to me, time after time, and asked to be allowed to go in for at least one play.

"I'm saving you," I said.

This didn't hold him. Back he came, pleading to get into the game, overlooking the fact that if he had been vitally important he would not have to apply; also that he was a sophomore with two years of play ahead of him.

"I'm saving you," I said again.

In desperation, as he saw the third-string lads rush in for the final few minutes, he resumed his annoyance. By this time it became evident that this young man needed a quick clear lesson in deflation. The game ended. Morose, he trudged by my side as we left the field.

"The game's over," he complained. "The season's over. What are you saving me for?"

"The Junior Prom," I said.

A wisecrack — if you call it that — of this type is a necessary adjunct to a coach's oral contacts with his players. Youngsters in their late teens and early twenties take more meaning from a pointed quip than from prolonged preachment, and if a coach seeks a sure way to have control of his boys, he'll be quicker if not sharper-tongued than they are.

One of the best nifties uttered at the right moment by a big league coach, assuaged the grief of his own team and smoothed the ruffled feelings of its opponents and prevented a possible rift in relations. Wisconsin was playing Minnesota. The score was 12 to 6 in favor of Minnesota. In the last minute of play Wisconsin tried a long pass, which a Minnesota back knocked down; but the field judge ruled that a Minnesota man had interfered illegally with the receiver. Wisconsin was given the decision and the score became a tie. There were growls and murmurs. The captains of the two teams, as per custom, claimed the ball. There was an impasse, which Coach Spears of Minnesota good-humoredly solved by remarking, "Give the ball to the field judge. He won the game."

This same member of the coaching fraternity created a laugh that resounded through all the territory of the Big Ten in another game with Wisconsin. Notre Dame had played the Cardinals at Madison with the famous Jack Elder in our backfield. As everybody knows, Elder was the boy who beat the Army in the fall of '29 with a 96-yard run of astonishing speed on a frozen field. For a back, Elder was light — 160 pounds, but a flash in action, one of America's best sprinters. When Notre Dame took the field against Wisconsin for this game, the grass on the gridiron was unusually long.

Some of our friends grumbled that the grass had been allowed to grow long purposely to hamper Elder's running. This was wrong. It didn't bother Elder at all — not any more than the Wisconsin players. However, the rumbling got into the press, and one newspaper man misquoted me in a witticism in which I was supposed to have admonished my players to be careful to keep the grass out of their eyes while looking for forward passes on defense. My own impression is that Wisconsin's playing field had a weak sod and they were trying to save it.

Coach Spears of Minnesota put the finishing touch to it. Playing Wisconsin after us on the same field, he crawled on hands and knees — before the game — through the same grass. Newspaper men asked what he was doing, and he replied, "I'm looking for a pair of Rockne's halfbacks who've been missing since Notre Dame played here."

Every good coach I know spices his relations with his own personnel, with his opponents and with officials, by using the flavor of humor. The student body is full of it — sometimes too full of it. As when the Carlisle Indians went down to play St. Louis to be welcomed by the St. Louis rooters with the spectacle of a funeral hearse containing a cigar-store Indian, followed by a cortege of wailing mourners. A boomerang joke, for it infuriated the braves, who beat a superior team by three to nothing.

In the thousand and one details of contact with everybody connected with the sport, unless the coach has a saving grace of humor, he is certainly to be counted among the lost. I've known of rivalries between star players that would inevitably have developed into bad blood — jeopardizing the prospects of the team and breaking the morale of the entire squad and student body by producing factions and cliques — unless the coach employed good humor plus firmness in handling the situation.

Two of the finest players that ever wore the blue and gold of Notre Dame provoked a situation where my fairly well-trained patience became exhausted.

They were Johnny Mohardt and Norm Barry. Mohardt was the most industrious of players. He was always first man out to practice and last man in. He tried hard to make the team in 1919, but wasn't quite good enough. In the spring of 1920, it was reported to me that Mohardt would spend hours on the practice field alone, trying to specialize in blocking. He had heard in campus gossip that I was on the lookout for an A-1 blocker for George Gipp. Mohardt became that blocker, and, in addition, he developed into an accurate forward passer.

But Barry, not so hard-working, was brilliant in his way. Uncertain as to the ability of either boy to sustain his quality through the season, I decided to alternate them as halfbacks. This made them rivals. In a game with Nebraska, Barry played well; Mohardt lagged. Then in a game with Army, Mohardt shone while Barry looked poor. Things reached an impasse when the two boys were glaring at each other during practice the Monday following the Army game. So I called them out and ordered them to return their suits.

Realizing that this was too severe punishment — banishment from the squad — for two boys whose offending arose from their eagerness to shine for their school, I relented. On Friday before the Indiana game, they were told they could rejoin the squad. Reports had come to me that the two had been near a fist fight on the campus, so it was up to me, as coach, to stop futher trouble. Yet there was a problem — how to balance them in the game for the benefit of the whole team. I started Mohardt and

Gipp. It was a game we expected to win easily. But Indiana gave us a surprise. At the end of the third period, the score was 10 to nothing against us, and George Gipp — our best offensive and defensive star — was injured.

The team didn't seem to be going anywhere. The only time any player was off his feet was when he was knocked down. What should I do? Suddenly I took Gipp out of the game.

"Barry, I called, "here's your chance. Go in there and insult them if you have to."

"Yeah," said Barry, tearing off his blanket, "and especially Mohardt."

Barry had no sooner taken position than the quarterback called Mohardt's number for an off-tackle play where Barry was supposed to block the end. Barry blocked him with a vengeance, carrying him almost to the bleachers on his back to let Mohardt through for an 18-yard gain.

On the next play it was Barry's turn to carry the ball. He said to Mohardt in the huddle, "Listen, you, take your end out the same way I did mine when I carry the ball or I'll sock you so hard on the jaw you'll have fallen arches."

The play came. Barry carried the ball — and Mohardt carried the end — out to where the head linesman carries the sticks. Barry gained 25 yards. Four more plays between those two and Notre Dame had a touchdown. The game was pulled out of the fire in the last minute by 13 to 10.

In the dressing room afterward I planned to make the boys shake hands. That was unnecessary. All the bile in their systems had been worked off clearing paths for each other to carry the ball. They've been the best of friends ever since.

Jack Cannon, the all-America guard, presented, for a brief time, one of those studies in temperament that a coach must gauge carefully before deciding whether or not he'll josh the player with a humorous sally or prod him with some other psychological weapon. Everybody who saw the 1929 game between

Army and Notre Dame will remember the bareheaded guard who happened to be in every spot where he was most needed to stop the Army ends and backs. By actual count Cannon took out more than 25 rushers that afternoon, gamboling like a lamb in pasture on a gridiron that was literally as hard as iron. Yet Cannon was not always a whirlwind at play. Even after he had made the team he seemed halted at times by lethargy. At practice before one of our biggest games the entire first string performed beautifully — with the exception of Cannon. This was on the day before the game. I was going to take him out of practice, but that might have been interpreted merely as a move to save him for the fame. Some sharper tactic was necessary. In the middle of the third practice period I called a halt.

"All right, boys," I said. "You might as well go to the showers now before Cannon spoils any more plays."

This had the effect of hitting Cannon with a brick — a psychological brick. He said nothing. I thought he might call at my home, as the boys sometimes do on the eve of a big game, to seek advice or argue with me. He didn't. This proved I had him sized up correctly.

Just before we went on the field for the game, I walked up to him where he stood calmly wondering whether or not he'd play.

"You go in with the first string, Cannon," I said.

His eyes lighted. When the first string was summoned for action, Cannon went in — and what a job he did! The gentlemen of the visiting team said afterward they were highly honored to have had a presidential salute of at least 21 cannons!

Just as in the classroom, so in managing college athletes, firmness and consideration and the knack of letting the boy know that you know his capacities and failings better than he does — win implicit confidence for the coach. Boys are generous in their loyalty when they are convinced of your fairness. Of course, they are not always convinced; but the boy who is not reasonable enough to see that the team counts for more than the individual, is not worth worrying about. He'll get his hardest lessons out of school.

As a shining example of unselfish effort for the team, I always recall the work of a lad whom the sportswriters dubbed Johnny "One-Play" O'Brien. With the score 6 to 6 in the Loyola game in 1928, O'Brien caught two passes and won the game.

In the Army game of that same year at Yankee Stadium, two dogged foes had fought their hearts out, and with just a few minutes to play the score stood 6 to 6. Notre Dame had the ball on the Army 40-yard line, second down, ten to go. Jack Chevigny had just been removed from the game, exhausted, which meant that our running attack could no longer function. It was time to gamble. I called for O'Brien and said:

"All right, Johnny. Out you go!" Nothing more.

Carideo, the quarterback, saw him and in spite of what stupid critics may say, it was not necessary for any message from the coach to inspire Carideo to call for the right play.

O'Brien had a specialty in which he excelled — a particularly pet pass play which he and John Niemiec, the halfback, had worked often in practice. It didn't require any masterminding on the part of Carideo to call for it. On the crack of the whip, O'Brien started down the field, veered to the left and then suddenly cut toward the right-hand corner of the field. He received the forward pass, ran for the touchdown and was promptly withdrawn.

O'Brien was six feet four and had an unusually long reach. This made him an ideal receiver. For the brunt of the game, he was unsuited. When he realized this, he took his role as a one-play man with splendid spirit — went into each game, took the pass aimed at him, and came out. The play in which he figured was always picturesque, unusually sensational: the crowds, for that reason, always expected more of him. But O'Brien contentedly did his job and sacrificed his personal ambition for the good of his side.

That, perhaps, is the best contribution football makes to character-building. It teaches the boys the necessity and value of cooperation and self-sacrifice. As boys, they will, of course, be boys. The coach's problem is to train them not to be too boyish in the sense of being too selfish.

To make the team and to stay with it, they must submit to regulation of their personal habits. In diet, all pastry is banned. Fruit replaces it, to supply alkaline balance. The diet for the Notre Dame squad — for all Notre Dame athletes in training — is scientifically prescribed. They eat meat once a day, roast beef preferred. They can have coffee only once, for breakfast. We insist on nine hours' sleep — all lights out at 10 p.m. There is no toleration of smoking or drinking in any form, for they most certainly diminish the efficiency of youth. On Fridays before games, and on Sundays after games, the boys are encouraged to eat liberally of figs and dates to supply sugar which is concentrated energy.

Rarely does a boy break the rules. He knows they are meant for his good. He knows, also, that he is never threatened. Action quickly follows default, where threats mean nothing. I remember a baseball coach who said he'd fire any boy off the team who left the hotel to visit a soda fountain late at night. Result: the whole team marched out in a body and had ice cream sodas. The coach was helpless — his authority impaired.

The Notre Dame boys see me smoke, and they know my answer to the old taunt: Don't do as I do, do as I say. It all depends on who you are, and what you're planning to do. A doctor advising a diabetic to avoid sugars doesn't need to follow the same advice.

My policy has always been to be firm rather than strict, to act rather than talk. It builds the best morale.

Walking through South Bend one afternoon, I saw a boy — in the old days before Prohibition — come out of a saloon. He was one of the best, and the only good hurdler on our track team. On investigation, I learned it was his habit to take a drink, usually beer, now and again. He may have done it again — but not as an athlete. When he was suddenly dropped from the squad, everybody rushed in consternation to my office to ask why.

"Ask him," I said.

It was a long time before it was necessary to discipline another boy for breaking training rules.

COACHING MEN

Psychology has its place in football, but not to the extent many football fans believe, otherwise schools would profit more by turning over the coach's job to the professor of philosophy. When I hear the football coach of some mental capacity referred to as a deep and serious thinker, as a master mind who evolves game-winning strategy that by a single brain-wave conquers tremendous opposition, pardon me if I smile. My mind goes back to one of the most dramatic flashes of gridiron intelligence in the hitherto unrecorded annals of the game.

In a non-college town in the Wabash Valley there was an outbreak of football fever. It reached its crisis in a love affair between the town belle and two young men who had spent four years in high school and about 10 years thereafter talking about their prowess as substitute backs on the high school team.

One was named Joe, and he was principally distinguished for the most artistic chrysanthemum haircut in the county. The other was named Ed, and he planned to be a dentist if his dad didn't insist on his going to a veterinary college.

Joe wanted to show the girl that his recital of his high school achievements was more authentic and glowing than Ed's. Ed, likewise, desired to demonstrate that his record had been better than Joe's.

Ed was the more resourceful — at first. He organized a football club and called it after the town. They met two or three local towns and vanquished them in contests evidently staged to determine who knew least about the game. This enterprise on Ed's part made him solid with the girl. Joe was about to be shelved, when he had a mental attack, and a subtle one. Shut out of organizing another football team in the town to rival Ed's — for Ed's outfit, after winning three games straight, received enthusiastic endorsement from the Chamber of Commerce — Joe went to a nearby town. Among other resources this town was famous as the seat of the county home for the feeble-minded. Joe sold the authorities the idea that football would be an excellent thing for the inmates. He was promptly appointed coach, manager and quarterback. Almost as promptly he issued a challenge to Ed's club, which was accepted. The day came when grandstands were filled to overflowing, and Joe's team of queer ducks lined up against Ed's combination of local talent. To make the occasion colorful, the girl sat in a field box and Ed wore a bright red sweater to baffle the players from the nut college.

Through three quarters the teams played each other to a standstill. Excitement was immense, and while orthodox football was more or less pushed into the discard, all the customers had a good time. Between Joe and Ed, however, there was more than a mere game at stake. The winner of the contest would also — by the laws of romance — be winner of the girl.

They redoubled their efforts in the final quarter, driving their teams on with inspirational cries and nifty slugging in the scrimmages. In a burst of energy, Ed got the upper hand on a fumble by an asylum player who imagined he was a Spanish ring bull and dropped the ball to charge at Ed's red sweater.

Ed's team scored a touchdown. Only five minutes remained to play, and Joe's forces were furious. Precious seconds slipped by. Defeat stared Joe in the face — almost as mockingly as Ed's bright red sweater.

Joe had another brain wave. On the sideline was a member of the nut college rooters, hissing and pumping his arms, giving a perfect imitation of a Big Four locomotive. Indeed, had you asked this gentleman what he was he would have replied that he was a Big Four Locomotive. As a matter of fact he had been an engine driver until a fireman did something unfriendly with a shovel.

Calling time out, Joe went to the sideline and addressed the human locomotive.

"Special ordered down the line," he said, "from Logansport to Wabash. Steam's up and we're ready to go."

The big fellow followed Joe on the field, and took his position as fullback. Joe cried signals, got the ball and passed it to the newcomer.

"Green lights," he thundered. "Blow the whistle, let her go!"

For a moment only the human locomotive stood, while Ed's players and spectators marveled in anticipation at what was about to occur. The fellow hissed, spouted sounds like escaping steam, pumped his arms like pistons and with a mighty roar started down the field. Players dropped in his wake. Only Ed finally remained, his bright red sweater a target in the sun. Ed was stunned. The human locomotive ate up the yards, and behind him, his chrysanthemum head butting over any opposition players who were indiscreet enough to arise, Joe charged on triumphant.

All appeared lost for Ed. The human locomotive was 20 yards away, 15, 12. Then Ed had a masterful inspiration — the sort that can come only to the naturally great psychologist. As the human locomotive, eyes fixed ahead at the goal line, came snorting up — huge and irresistible — Ed didn't tackle. He tore off his red sweater, made a noise like a fog horn, waved the sweater in the breeze. The human locomotive applied brakes, stood still, then shunted back — back — back, trampling Joe and his chrysanthemum haircut in his reversed path, until he wound up with a safety and two more points for Ed.

While, as they say in Wall Street, I have the facts of this unique play on good authority, I cannot guarantee them. Still, the story illustrates the highly dramatic brand of psychology which the master football coach is supposed to have at his fingertips. In which case, I can not pretend to qualify as a master coach. A smart running backfield — I've discovered — is better than any number of psychologists in winning football games.

Yet psychology is very important to the coach in his relations with his players, his opponents and the alumni who seem to be so influential with both. He must have some understanding of the minds of various types of boys if he is to elicit the best there is in any boy who tries to make the football grade. He must also understand public opinion regarding the school and its athletic reputation, as it exists in the community where the school is located. Likewise, he must — if he wants to be successful or even to hold his job — analyze the alumni attitude and decide when he should give them what they want and when he should oppose them for wanting too much. A great deal of the coach's work and more than a great deal of the coach's woes await him far from the gridiron's madding crowds.

Just before game time, a good football coach knows what the physical condition of his boys is. He knows just about how much football they know mentally. But there's one thing he does not know — what's in their hearts. Generally this is most important of all.

The football coach must know the emotional reactions of every one of his boys. He must furnish tests so that he can find out before the big games all about the psychological processes of every individual upon whom he relies, or he's in for some disappointing shocks.

Every season, for instance, I find material that shines on the practice field, but falls down in the test of a real game. Last year I had a typical case. A western youngster had all the earmarks of a great broken-field runner for the halfback spot. He was a sensation in practice games where visiting alumni saw him. The same alumni wondered why this lad was never used in big games. It was because he failed in small games. When he got the ball, he tightened up, lost control of his nerves as the grandstand bellowed, and also lost his speed. He received innumerable chances. It wasn't his fault. Yet, although he never played in a major game to win his letter, that lad did a very real service for the school because his fleetness as a ball carrier in practice games gave the first team first class opposition.

The opposite psychological case to the practice athlete is the firing line competitor. We meet several of these each season. In his way, George Gipp was one. By firing line competitor, I mean a lad who may be indifferent during tests and tryouts, but who comes through in the acid test of competition against quality.

In 1928, Jack Elder, fastest of Notre Dame backs, fumbled half the time he carried the ball in practice games. He was weak on forward pass defense; he couldn't block. But out in California, the last game that year, he found himself. It will be remembered that his most spectacular play in 1929 was a forward pass he stole from the Army to turn it into a one-man touchdown. Elder had become a firing line competitor. Jack Chevigny, a great Notre Dame halfback, and our backfield coach at present, used to give an imitation of Leon Errol when he was with the scrubs. His idea of a broken-field run was to trip on a blade of grass and fall prostrate. But he came through splendidly when the big games stirred his heart.

About the worst dub I have ever encountered in a practice game was Johnny Weibel. He was one of the greenest chaps I ever saw come out on our field. But he was a strong boy, so we used him in the scrubs, although he impressed me as being preternaturally lazy. I studied him for a long time and decided that Johnny had contempt for practice. He evidently figured —

as most competitors do — that he should save his energy for the real games. And this almost defeated his ambition, for it is doubtful if Weibel would have had a chance to play for Notre Dame in fast company. He had been relegated to a third-string guard. Even then I was disinclined to use him. But in a game with Army, Harvey Brown, a regular guard, had his elbow twisted in a play and was yanked out. The second-string guard withstood three hard plays and limped off the field with a sprained ankle. Having nothing else to do I sent in Weibel.

Smythe was the Army quarterback — and a right smart one. He must have seen my stoic look of disappointment when two guards came to the injured bench one after the other. Army was battering its way toward our goal line at the time. They were about 12 yards from a touchdown when Weibel went in. I watched the play closely, and saw Weibel crouch low, teeth gritted when Smythe shot a play at him. Army gained a little. Smythe tried another spot in the line and gained more. Then he went back to Weibel with the ball on Notre Dame's 4-yard line and massed mobs yelling for a score. Weibel steadied himself for the shock and stopped the Army's charge. It was fourth down, two to go. Smythe smiled. I knew his next play would go right at Weibel. It did — and what a pile-driving smash! I expected to see Weibel flat and finished. The whistle blew and there was Weibel — the Army back prostrate before him and the ball still two yards from Notre Dame's goal.

An assortment of teams using different styles of attack and defense give a coach plenty of opportunity to test the qualifications of different players — especially those whose temperament he finds it not so easy to analyze.

Take the boy who is so high-strung and nervous that from Wednesday on he cannot sleep for worrying over the coming game. What shall be done with him? A good coach tells him on Wednesday that he's not going to play. The high-strung lad is disappointed and naturally sullen or resentful — but he relaxes and sleeps well at night. Twenty minutes before game time the coach tells him, "I've changed my mind. You're going in."

Immediately the lad becomes high-strung and keyed up — but this is the proper time for that. The coach might also keep this fellow out of the game until, we'll say, the start of the second quarter.

Then there is the big, powerful, phlegmatic chap who just will not put out, will not become aggressive and cross the line of scrimmage. He is just too friendly with everybody to play football well, and, in business later on, will probably get to be known as a good-natured sap. What can be done to arouse this lad from his self-satisfied, lethargic state of mind? A good coach will go to him just before the big game and say, "Clarence, your teammates and the student body and the alumni think you're afraid. I'm the only friend you've got. I'm sticking with you and putting you in that game today. Now what are you going to do? Show me up? And have these other people give us the horse laugh?"

If the lad has any character at all the result will be an irresistible, pile-driving, headlong charging, irrepressible fighting machine who will surprise everyone, and himself most of all, by what he can actually do when fired up. Many big linemen have found themselves by this process. Later on, when they go out to play the big game of life where the rewards go only to those who excel, he enters with the spirit of confidence that he's just as good as the other fellow and that he can do a thing if he will.

When he has a practical knowledge of the psychology of his own players the coach's mental equipment is still far from complete unless he learns something of the temperament or psychological mannerisms of players — particularly of star players — who are on teams he is to oppose.

One of the most versatile and dangerous Army men was Light Horse Harry Wilson, the charging halfback. He played havoc with our line because he mastered a feinting getaway that was hard to stop once it was started. Our problem was to reach Mr.

Wilson before he could start. I observed that Wilson had a habit of blushing just before he went into action, which led to the belief that the calling of his number by the quarterback tautened his nervous system. Our own line was warned to watch him closely. Sure enough, whenever Wilson flushed, it was just before he charged through with the ball. Even with this tip-off it was hard enough to arrest his progress; before we learned this symptom of his impending activity we had lost many, many yards.

The institution known as "scouting" is supposed to be a source of all necessary information about his opponents to the varsity coach. His scouts are supposed to tell him of new trick plays, of the idiosyncrasies of star players on opposing teams, of everything from the state of the ground to the condition of the cheerleaders' tonsils. Enthusiastic alumni of a school are often self-appointed football scouts. As a rule, their enthusiasm is in inverse ratio to their knowledge of the game and their powers of observation in spotting innovations or clever deceptions in the play of the schools they are scouting. Unless an old player of mine or somebody well qualified to see and report sends me news regarding an opposing team, I am not at all disturbed. When an old college pal of mysterious mien tells me that so-and-so of such-and-such a team raises his right eyebrow just before taking the ball for an end run, I raise my right eyebrow and let it go at that.

Back in 1915 when I was assistant to Jess Harper, part of my job was to do his scouting. We were to play Nebraska, and so Jess wired Jumbo Steihn, Nebraska coach, that I was going out to scout their Kansas-Aggie game. I did.

I came back with two mysterious bits of information.

Nebraska's great threat was a fine halfback named Chamberlin. In the Kansas-Aggie game, he scored touchdown after touchdown on wide end runs. I came back with the startling information that Chamberlin could not and did not cut back at any time.

What happened when Notre Dame played Nebraska? Right near the end of the first half Nebraska had the ball on our 40-yard line. Chamberlin took it on the next play. Our players all swung wide, over-committing themselves to what we thought we knew of the runner's habitual tactics. To our surprise, Chamberlin cut back, and with no Notre Dame player in front of him, he ran 40 yards for a touchdown. I was responsible for that touchdown, not the Notre Dame team.

The second bit of startling information I conveyed to our boys was this: this man Chamberlin was left-handed. I told our boys when he licked his fingers he always forward passed. When he did not lick his fingers, he always ran. What happened? Right near the end of the game, the score was tied 13 to 13. The ball was in midfield in Nebraska's possession. Back it came to Chamberlin, who started off as if on an end run. Suddenly he stopped, whirled and threw a long pass to Nebraska's right end, who caught the ball and ran for a touchdown. Where was our halfback assigned to cover him? He had seen that Chamberlin did not lick his fingers. Therefore, feeling sure it was to be a run, up he came, with disastrous results to Notre Dame. Chamberlin had crossed us up. I lost that game, not the Notre Dame team. The final score was 20 to 19 in favor of Nebraska.

In the fall of 1926, a scout reported to me that Carnegie Tech was ordinary against West Virginia, which sized up as strong opposition at that time. My plans made it necessary for me to be in Chicago at a Big Ten Conference and the Army-Navy game on the day we met Carnegie Tech. Down in Pittsburgh, our boys were prepared for the usual tough battle. They got an unusually tough one. Carnegie Tech had been playing possum for the scout I sent there, holding Harpster, their bright, particular star, under wraps. He cut loose like a thunderbolt against us.

Sitting between Tad Jones and Pop Warner at the Army-Navy game, I received a wire from Pittsburgh. It bore the doleful news that Carnegie Tech had beaten a great Notre Dame team 19 to nothing.

"Too bad," said Pop Warner.

"Tough luck," commiserated Tad Jones.

"Come behind the stands," I invited both, "and give me the kicking I deserve."

These tips from volunteer scouts are invariably misleading. Indeed, about the most informative thing volunteers from the alumni ever report about the opposite team is that it generally plays with 11 men. In 1920, a friend tipped us off that Northwestern's defensive left halfback had a glass eye where his good right eye should have been. This was confirmed when he took the field, so our tactic was to daze him with forward pass plays. Northwestern promptly substituted, and we had to switch to running plays just as we had relied upon putting the game in the bag with quick aerial flings.

But scouting — and the tricks of the trade — work both ways. In our 1929 season many Notre Dame enthusiasts wondered why our forward pass game was not very much in evidence. I knew, although ill in bed, that they were scouting all our major games — and we won all of our earlier ones without the pass. That was kept under cover until we met Southern California. Their scouts reported that Notre Dame's pass game was of no consequence. But we completed five long passes that won the game.

So, too — again earlier in my acquaintance with what scouting can do to fool both friend and foe — in 1921 we played exceptionally orthodox football. For a purpose. Our leading opponent was the Army, which believed what its scouts reported — that our game was strictly orthodox. This, in turn, meant that we would follow the rules that guide smart teams and never dream of passing in our own territory. When the Army halfbacks, observing our orthodox game, stayed up to the line of scrimmage, they remained there once too long. Paul Castner, our fullback, faked a line plunge, but instead the quarterback passed the ball to Johnny Mohardt who shot it 40 yards to Roger Kiley who raced 30 yards for a touchdown.

And while scouting has brought me — as it brings every coach — disappointments, I've had valuable tips that helped to win games. In 1924, we learned through the scout route that Carnegie Tech had adopted a man-to-man defense, and that the center, fullback, left halfback and quarterback were fast runners. Their right half was a grand blocker but a slow runner. Play during the first half verified all this. So Crowley was sent into the defense right halfback's territory where he ran him ragged all afternoon, catching all the passes Stuhldreher sent his way.

The same game produced another illustration of the usefulness of legitimate scouting. Their center, a most ubiquitous young man, had been a thorn in the side of all of Tech's opponents. However, this is what our scout discovered in analyzing his play: his forte was to stand out of position, teasing the offensive quarterback to call a play at the apparent weakness and then, as the play started, he would move and correct this. For instance, he would line up on the scrimmage line and the offensive quarterback would think, "Now is the chance to throw a short pass over the middle of the line." The play would be called. The offensive team's right end would cut over in the middle territory, which had apparently been wide open, to catch the pass, and lo and behold, the Carnegie center was back there jumping for the ball! Or the center would line up four yards behind the line of scrimmage, leaving what appeared to be a big gap in the center of the Carnegie Tech line. The offensive quarterback would call for a line plunge or a cutback through the same hole. There would be little or no gain, because at the snap of the ball, the Carnegie center would dash up to the line of scrimmage, filling the gap and piling up the play.

When we played them, in the second half, the astute Stuhldreher just kept crossing this center, with the result that

Notre Dame scored four touchdowns in the third quarter.

Football science has a place for legitimate scouting, just as it has a place for psychology, but where the emphasis is overlayed, these by-issues of the game defeat their own ends. Really, the thing that is wrong with scouting is the word *scouting.* I suggest that in its stead we use the word research, or, as it might better be defined — the making of every game a football clinic. Everybody in every game is interested in what others do with it, especially when those others are future opponents at the game. When scouting is done over and aboveboard, and one school announces it will have an official representative to see a public exhibition by another school, we all know where we stand. Then there can be no innuendo that there was secret scouting, spying or other betrayal of confidence.

We are all curious as to what our competitors are doing. The city editor of the *New York Times* is most interested in the first edition of the *New York Herald-Tribune.* The grocer on one corner wants most to know what his rival on the other corner is going to sell certain lines at; physicians in a community are most eager to know what new therapeutic apparatus some professional brother is introducing; and department store heads are persistently inquisitive as to what their competitors will have a sale in next. So research men are continually finding out what additions to scientific knowledge are being made by other research men — and increasing or improving the discoveries of others.

Why should not this same process prevail in football?

Naturally, a coach's ingenuity in improvising new plays is part of his assets. He can't patent his inventions, but he should be protected by mutual trust. Really, there are no new plays any more than in humor there are any new jokes. All are variations of old principles — but it is in the new touch, in the novel ways of performing old plays, in new deceptive tactics applied to old routines, that the surprise element, which is the best stuff in football is to be found.

The most loyal support a coach can have — support he should cherish and hold — should come from the student body. When the coach knows his business that support is never failing. Faculty may criticize, alumni may criticize, newspapers and neighbors — but never have I heard the student body criticize in either victory or defeat.

Yet of late there has been detected a tendency, especially in élite schools, to substitute social life with caste implications, for athletic prestige and campus activity — a movement led by lounge lizards.

Several years ago out at Notre Dame a group of mezzanine-floor high hurdlers presented as their candidate for president of the senior class one of the nicest boys that ever appeared on a campus. So nice, indeed, that whenever I met him I never knew whether to kiss him or slap him. The opposing candidate was a campus leader, not an athlete, but a real he-man mentally — an orator, debator and a hard worker in many extracurricular activities. But he waited tables. The pretty boy won in the election and Notre Dame had gone cake-eater.

To meet this situation, at the football mass-meeting the following fall I announced that Notre Dame, in harmony with the spirit prevailing on the campus as evidenced by the senior election, would pursue a new football policy. As the result of this policy, I said, in 1935 Notre Dame would play their highly-respected rival, Northwestern, as usual. However, I added, you boys will be alumni by that time, and those living far away and picking up the morning paper the day after the game, to read about it, will turn, not to the vulgar sporting sheet — oh, my, no — but to the society column. And the account will be somewhat as follows:

> "Receiving at fullback for Northwestern was M. Bickerdash Pix III, of the famous North Shore family. The entire Northwestern team was gaily clad in purple-mauvette

tunics, and about the waist was a white girdle with a Louis XIV buckle. The shoes were by Hanan and Son and the hosiery specially designed with beige tasseled garters by Patou — perfume by Houbigant.

"Kicking off for Notre Dame was T. Fitzpatrick Murphy, who is better known to his cronies as Two Lump, as he always asks for two lumps of sugar in his orange pekoe. The Notre Dame team also presented a striking appearance with their green shirt waists and their head-gear resembling a woodman's toque — giving a very neat appearance without being at all gaudy, although their hippads were trimmed with georgette. Hanging from the necks were pendants, lavalière type on which was engraved the motto of the university: 'Fight fairly but furiously.'

"Precisely at two-thirty the referee, dressed in regulation costume of plus fours and crêpe de Chine blouse, blew his whistle. Two Lump met the ball squarely and sent it soaring down the field right into the arms of Bickerdash, who, catching it, brought it back 5, 10, 15 yards before he was tagged by a deft tap on the shoulder by Nouveauriche Gilhooey, the Irish left end. Northwestern lined up and tried three running plays to no avail. Notre Dame's tagging defense was impregnable. So, on fourth down, old Bickerdash dropped back from a kick formation and sent a long spiral soaring 60 yards down the field to old Two Lump, who was tagged right in his tracks. He couldn't move.

"Then, as Notre Dame took the offensive with the ball, they found, to their dismay, that Northwestern was just as clever at defensive tagging as they were. As a result neither team could gain at all so all throughout the first half a punting duel resulted between old Two Lump and Bickerdash, neither gaining any advantage. Between halves both teams had tea. Refreshed therefrom, and inspired by words of wisdom from their respective professors of

THE GOLDEN DOME — The Golden Dome already reigned above the Notre Dame campus when a young Knute Rockne enrolled at the university in 1910. The dome, which is crowned by a nineteen-foot high statue of the Blessed Virgin, remains the centerpiece of the campus today.

AT PRACTICE — When he wasn't participating in the action, Rockne often coached practices from a favorite wooden chair.

NEW YORK STOCKS

STOCKBROKER — Rockne opened a stock brokerage firm in South Bend in 1930.

FRIEND OF THE MAYOR — *As Rockne's fame grew, he became as well known as such public figures as Mayor Jimmy Walker (left) of New York City.*

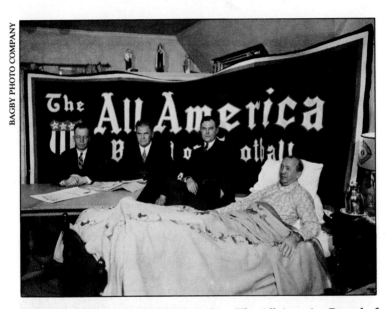

SELECTING ALL-AMERICANS — The All America Board of Football came to Rockne's sickbed so that he could participate in the selection of its 1929 All America team.

BAGBY PHOTO COMPANY

AN INSPIRATION AT PRACTICE — With their beloved coach seriously ill but still making every effort to contribute to his team, the Fighting Irish had to be inspired by his every visit to the practice field in 1929. No team ever made a greater effort for their coach than the Notre Dame team of 1929, which outscored its opponents 145–38 in nine wins on the road.

COURAGE ON THE SIDELINE — *Desperately ill with phlebitis, Rockne coached his team from his bed and from a wheelchair on several occasions in 1929. In a remarkable season in which the Irish played all their games on the road while Notre Dame Stadium was under construction, they won all nine games and the national championship.*

ONE OF THE FIRST FREQUENT FLIERS — As Rockne's
fame soared, his travel schedule grew hectic. In the early days of
commercial aviation, he became an enthusiastic air traveler.

THE LAST TELEGRAM — *Rockne sent this telegram to his wife, Bonnie, just hours before the plane crash which took his life.*

ROCKNE'S FUNERAL — *Sacred Heart Church, on the University of Notre Dame campus, was the setting for Knute Rockne's funeral on Saturday, April 4, 1931. Although only 1,400 of his friends and admirers could be seated inside the church, more than 100,000 lined the route from Notre Dame to Highland Cemetery, and millions more listened to the ceremonies on a coast-to-coast radio broadcast by the Columbia Broadcasting System.*

OUTSIDE THE CHURCH — *Ten thousand people listened to Rockne's funeral services on a public address system set up outside Sacred Heart Church.*

*KNUTE ROCKNE POSTAGE STAMP — On March 9, 1988,
President Ronald Reagan joined Rockne's daughter, Mrs. An-
thony Kochendorfer, and Rev. Edward A. Malloy, C.S.C, president of the University of Notre Dame, to dedicate a special Knute
Rockne commemorative stamp.*

THE ROCK — A bronze bust of Rockne, sculpted by Nison Tregor in 1940, greets visitors to the Knute Rockne Memorial Building at the University of Notre Dame.

THE ROCKNE MOTORCAR — Studebaker introduced a new automobile, the Rockne, in honor of the coach (photo courtesy of the Studebaker National Museum in South Bend, Indiana).

ROCKNE'S LEGACY — Rockne was one of the first coaches to establish coaching schools. Here, he conducts a summer coaching school at the University of Southern California. Many of his players followed in his footsteps to become coaches at the collegiate level.

A HERO TO THE BOYS OF AMERICA — *Many young boys in America dreamed of playing football for Knute Rockne and his Notre Dame Fighting Irish.*

psychology, both teams went back into the second half with renewed determination to do or die. But, lackaday, nothing startling happened all during the third quarter as both teams continued their rare defense of superb tagging!

"Up until within about five minutes of the end of the fourth quarter, it looked as though it were destined to be a tie game, which, you know, is so unsatisfactory.

"Suddenly out of a rhythmical gavotte, a sort of hidden-ball evolution, old Bickerdash broke loose and went streaking up the sidelines with a clear field to the goalposts. The Northwestern stands were mad with pandemonium; but in the Irish stands a deathly stillness because it looked like sure defeat for Notre Dame. But they failed to reckon on the resourcefulness and resiliency of mind of old Two Lump. Now when Two Lump, who was back playing safety, the last man on defense, saw Bickerdash streaking toward the goal line and no one there to stop him, did he give up and become panicky? Not old Two Lump. With a savoire-faire for which he was justly famous, he cupped his hands and he called in a loud clear voice that could be heard all over the amphitheater, 'I say, Bickerdash, old thing, there's a terrible run in your stocking.'

"Imagine the intense embarrassment and mortification of poor old Bickerdash. What could he do to hide his discomfiture but drop the ball and sneak away to the clubhouse, and the game was saved."

This story had the effect I hoped for, of restoring the normal balance in our masculine democracy, so that today, while social events have their place, they are not paramount and the old school continues to turn out men of culture, character and courage.

Next to faculty and student support, I'm strong for alumni enthusiasm. I'm equally strong for alumni pessimism. Indeed, in every town I like to establish a gloom alumnus — an honest chap who'll write me what's wrong with me and the football team and why and how we should be better. At the same time, I discourage the synthetic alumni from everywhere who particularly seem to follow the fortunes of Notre Dame in too robust a fashion. They mean well, but they could mean better by giving Notre Dame the benefit of their support without giving our opponents evidence of their disfavor.

About the biggest job any coach has on his hands is to take alumni enthusiasm and put it into right channels — to curb, for example, the zealous alumnus who takes it upon himself to visit the presidents of important schools and demand to know why they do not include his alma mater in their football schedule. The head of a great Eastern university once wrote me asking what he should do with such a fellow. I wired him forthwith, "Throw him out."

Toward the sempiternal alumnus who follows the team wherever it goes, pursuing its star players with a fervid friendliness, the coach must be more charitable. Notre Dame has several of these perpetual college boys on its roster of fans. One I know makes it his life work to follow the team. In a game once, remarkable for the verbal hostility leveled at our players, it didn't look as if we had a friend in the place, when suddenly a raucous voice began a series of one-man yells that let us know our alumni were not unrepresented. This one-man cheering section shouted so prodigiously that he won over a large number of neutrals and before the end of the game we were in possession of a lustily vocal proportion of the spectators.

This chap was a blessing. I have known alumni to be the opposite. When we played Indiana a few seasons back, it was hard going. The game should have been easily won, if comparative scores in past games meant anything — and, as a rule, they don't. But we had a much stronger team, which the Indiana boys, to their credit, were handily defeating. Sensing the loss of this annual game, the Notre Dame line stiffened, the backs rose in their might and we managed to squeeze through with a touch-down victory.

It seemed to me to be an occasion for rejoicing at the banquet following the game — which turned out to be one of the hardest-won victories on any of our schedules. I observed, however, that a few alumni at the dinner were anything but elated. Making inquiries I learned that these old grads had made considerable bets to the effect that their old school would win by at least three or four touchdowns. This was confirmed by the growlings of some of the disappointed gamblers.

When they called upon me for a speech that night, the boys got one. I was bristling and, I fear, laid into those inconsiderate chaps with a vehemence that shocked them. They were reminded that boys who went on the gridiron and gave the best there was in them were entitled to better than money support. Win, or lose, or draw, they should be cheered on during the game and after it by any man sharing loyalty to the school. And so forth. It didn't add to the harmony of the occasion, but it provided one fine chance for one coach to do what at some time or other every coach would like to do — put the gamblers in their place.

With the old grads and the neighbors, the coach must build goodwill for the benefit of his team. It's fatal to high-hat the people of the community where the school is located. Accept the support of Rotary, Kiwanis and the rest — they provide a background of enthusiasm which is bound to inspire the players. And welcome criticism.

I make it a rule never to take criticism too seriously. Walking into a barbershop a day or two after a game, especially a game in which we've been defeated, I find it takes the edge off everything to bow to the assembled barbers and customers and ask jovially, "Good morning. How are all the coaches today?"

No matter if the fans are alumni, neighbors or just plain

customers at the gates, they seem to like bigger and better scores. For my part, they'll get the best games that can be given by the material in hand. But it is folly to pile up scores at the expense of weak opponents just to gratify the vanity of followers. It's unfair to the opposite team, and to one's own players. A game won by a point is none the less won, and better to watch than a one-sided contest.

I have found that the best relations prevail when opposing teams are treated with scrupulous fairness. When they lose they appreciate not being martyrized to make a football holiday, and when they win there's nothing they admire more than an utter absence of alibis on the part of the defeated college and coach.

But in football, as in everything else, it's impossible to please everybody. Bask in the sunshine of a winning schedule, a difficult schedule — and those are the only schedules worthwhile, for "buffer" or rest games to induce a letdown that, in turn, brings casualties — win your way through a half a dozen tough assignments, and just as you are congratulating yourself on results, some busy soul is preparing a brickbat to aim at your lifted head.

Some day there will be an exhibit in some American museum. It will be the forlorn figure of the coach who pleased nobody. And next to it will be another — and more forlorn exhibit — the preserved remains of the coach who tried to please everybody.

THE LEGENDARY GEORGE GIPP

George Gipp was the greatest football player Notre Dame ever produced. He was unequaled in the game by anybody, save, perhaps, Jim Thorpe. Gipp was nature's pet and, as with many of her pets, nature also punished him. Gipp had everything to make a man great — splendid physique (he was six feet two and weighed 185 pounds), balanced temperament, a brilliant mind. He became great at the art he loved most — football. If his untimely end held a touch of tragedy, it was not because of any lack of mental or moral assets on his part, but because nature that had given to him so generously, denied him at the very peak of his career when he was to be crowned the outstanding all-America fullback.

I first met George Gipp on a football field. It was and is a habit of mine to ride or stroll to the practice field and observe groups of freshmen or nondescript students kicking footballs around. Once in a great while you can spot among these clumsy beginners genuine talent.

On this early autumn afternoon in 1916 the practice field was all but deserted. A tall lad in everyday campus clothes was booting a football to a boy in a playing suit who kicked it back. The uniformed lad was a candidate for the freshman team.

Their play seemed nothing more than a casual duel of punts between a football aspirant and some hall friend or roommate who had come out to oblige.

The style of the taller boy caught my eye. He picked up the ball, poised his body with natural grace, slid the ball to the ground and drop-kicked with perfect ease — 50 yards! For about 10 minutes I watched him. His kicks were far and placed evidently where he wanted them to go to give the other player catching practice. Here, I thought, was somebody worth examining. When he strolled from the field as if bored, I stopped him.

"What's your name?" I asked.

Most freshmen regard the football coach as if he's a deity on duty for the season. This boy was almost indifferent.

"Gipp," he said. "George Gipp. I come from Calumet."

"Played high school football?" I asked.

"No," he said. "Don't particularly care for football. Baseball's my dish."

"What led you to come to Notre Dame?" I asked.

"Friends of mine are here," he said.

"Put on a football suit tomorrow," I invited, "and come out with the freshmen scrubs. I think you'll make a football player."

The lad with Gipp stared pop-eyed.

"Why," he said, "he's been kicking those punts and drops with ordinary low shoes. What'll he do with football boots?"

That question was soon answered. Gipp romped through the freshman line on the very first play of a scrub game, the first time he had ever carried a ball in competition under the coach's eye. I learned that he had gone out for the Brownson Hall team, the usual thing for boys to do at Notre Dame, as every student physically capable of doing so is expected to enroll in his hall squad. But Gipp was not interested, and had quit the hall team.

After a month of knocking about with the freshmen, in which I observed him four or five times and watched how naturally he acquired running, kicking and tackling technique, we sent him into his first game. It was against Western State Normal, tough competition for any bunch of freshmen. The game was tied up in the last three minutes. Gipp had been doing a great deal of ball carrying, showing a lot he had learned and a lot he needed to learn — principally cutting back and interfering at which he was weak. In one of those frown-faced huddles dear to all freshman teams, Gipp insisted that he be allowed to try a kick to win three points and the game. His quarterback and captain argued against it. The quarterback called for a punt, as a matter of fact, to get the ball out of his own territory and make sure of a draw when a win seemed impossible.

Gipp took the ball and fell back to his own 38-yard line. With effortless grace he drop-kicked the ball and it soared high and away, parting the square of space above the crossbar. A perfect bid for the three points that won the game.

This Frank Merriwell finish — disregarding signals, to win a game — was so poetically right that I thought Gipp too good to be true. He himself seemed to have no thought about the matter. Where another boy would be flushed in triumph, this youngster took congratulations calmly. Even when I asked him to come out in the next practice between varsity and scrubs he showed no emotion.

"All right," he said. "If you think I can do any good."

In this game the scrubs were to represent the Army. Good scrub players had been schooled to imitate the styles of various Army stars. But I had found nobody on either varsity or scrub squads who could give an imitation of Elmer Oliphant, the groundgaining Army jehu. This was why I wanted Gipp. For three days I took him personally in hand, making him vary his pace, break his runs and cut back and dodge. He was extremely patient, even during the dull repetition of slow motion of every part of a long broken-field run. Next he was initiated into Oliphant's veering style of ball-carrying which arched his body so that he could spin or pivot at any fraction of an instant.

The varsity knew Gipp was going to be sent in against them. They were primed to stop him. They didn't. Gipp gave a perfect imitation of Oliphant and ran wide around end, passing the secondary defense with ease and scoring a touchdown. It was splendid vindication of my faith in the boy's ability. The only drawback was that in the actual game with Army, Oliphant gave a perfect imitation of Gipp and also made an end run for a touchdown.

Becoming in his freshman year a hero of campus talk is enough to inflate any youngster's head. But this boy Gipp had the superb personal policy of being indifferent to everything. Even on my short acquaintance with him this caused me to marvel. The explanation came, quite dramatically, later.

He reported to me that he would have to work his way through school. There were a few jobs of the white-collar type available. Those who had them to give would have been glad to have hired a boy who, in his freshman year, was already an accepted football hero in a school that had no small reputation for football heroes.

Gipp made his own choice. "I want to wait on tables," he said.

He became a hash-slinger and a most efficient one. Visitors to the refectory were surprised to have Gipp pointed out to them — after his fame became more than Midwestern — wearing a white waiter's coat and passing out tureens of soup and plates of stew. But the two tables in his charge — waiters nearest the kitchen had to cover two tables — were always promptly served and promptly cleared. He took the job seriously because it paid for his room and board. Once, when a New England lad received a hamper of lobsters — an unusual delicacy in our part of the Midwest — Gipp found a way to serve the jumbos without benefit of claw crackers. He broke every claw between his strong fingers.

My fear for Gipp was that nature had made him such a fine athlete that, over-gifted, he would not appreciate or respect his gifts. He lived quietly, had few companions — apparently cared nothing for female company, of which there's none whatever on the Notre Dame campus. He skipped the study room more frequently than I liked to see him do. But a check-up on his habits showed him with fewer than the usual faults of star athletes.

During his first summer he surpassed everybody as an outfielder and hitter in freshman baseball. There, as in football, he early showed a tendency to dominate quietly but effectively. He had a keen sense of strategy. I didn't see this game; but I was told that once when he was sent in with orders to make a bunt he slugged the ball for a home run, and explained that the afternoon was much too hot to be running around bases. He had a fine throwing arm — shooting the ball from boundary to plate on one hop.

What I hoped would be the hallmark of quality in the athlete who seemed too good to be true, namely, humor, was lacking in his early months at school. He was pleasant without being cheerful, affable without being congenial. He appeared just too sure of himself.

In his first year of gridiron play we held him under leash. We had plenty of stars, and as he was only 22, and the war was on, it was my policy to save him for the 1918 season. At that time it looked as if all our first-string men would join the service. That's exactly what happened. After a brief season that did not officially count as a scholastic year in 1918, Gipp, while having an opportunity to show that his greatness was growing, was not given too many chances to shine. 1918 was my first year as head coach, and I made it my undeviating rule to handle the boys without in the least putting anybody in a spot where I might be suspected of favoritism.

Gipp joined the Students' Army Training Corps, which some cynics irreverently paraphrased as Safe At The College. But he and most of the other lads in the Corps were too young for service.

When he returned to school after the holidays he switched his course from Arts and Letters to Law. Which meant nothing to me so long as he studied. I hope I'm pardoned for speaking in this proprietary or, at least, paternal way of the boy, because I felt the thrill that comes to every coach when he knows it is his fate and his responsibility to handle unusual greatness — the perfect performer who comes rarely more than once in a generation.

This year, 1919, I felt would be a great one for Gipp. During early spring practice he displayed uncanny accuracy in kicking and blocking. I should have mentioned that he had shown the football intuition that no coach or system can teach in the first major game in which he had appeared for long — against Army at West Point in 1917. We had the Army beaten 7 to 2 as we came to the last few minutes of play. The cadets cut loose and marched to the tune of several first downs, planting the ball on our 20-yard line. There they were held, but advanced for the fourth and final down to our 8-yard line. Remember the score was 7 to 2.

Gipp remembered it. Army's quarterback barked signals and they lined up for a placekick. Gipp instantly cried, "Look out for a pass!"

He was right. Army didn't kick. They gambled for six points instead of an almost certain three. Six points would have won the game. But Gipp warned our defense in time. Receivers were covered and he himself knocked the pass down and saved the game.

That was quick-thinking. It made him, as far as I was concerned. I knew there'd be nothing to stop this man being the outstanding star of his next full season. Nothing, that is, except Gipp.

One bright spring morning in 1920, I received the encouraging news — the news that puts a coach beside himself — that his bright particular star had been fired from school. Gipp was kicked out for missing too many classes. It seemed too late to do anything except scold him, and that was profitless. Yet, when I tackled him on his remissness and told him that he had put the finish to, not on, a brilliant athletic career, he quietly asked me why he couldn't have an oral examination. Townsmen of South Bend even appealed to the school authorities to give Gipp another chance. Gipp claimed to have been ill and he got it on that account.

Gipp went into that examination room with the whole school and the whole city waiting on the outcome. Some of his inquisitors were no football fans. They were prepared to stop his scholastic run with tough tackling questions and blocking from the books. His professors knew that Gipp was no diligent student. He made no notes. But he astonished everybody by what he knew when it came to cross-examination. He passed back into school, and there was general rejoicing. Not, however, by Gipp. Calmly, as usual, he accepted victory; but it was observed that he was once more regular in attending class.

The boy was really a master showman, with a mind alert to catch every effective detail of a show. Secretly, although he gave no outward sign, he loved the dramatic. To him it was striking fun to be fired from school because he wouldn't study, only to be returned when it was discovered, under fire, that he knew quite as much as the most unwearying plodders. The lad had brilliance, a sense of dramatic opportuneness, of doing the right unpreconceived thing at exactly the right, unpreconceived moment that made me wonder, at times, what self-dramatizing leaders of men must have been among his forebears. Even Gipp's voice was a warm, vibrant baritone, full of life. Yet his ancestry, so far as I knew, was Puritan. His father was a Congregational minister.

This detail, mentioned by him when he applied for a change

of domicile at the university, led to one of his crisp comebacks. A dormitory mate, chiding Gipp as a meek heretical lamb among orthodox wolves, was surprised when Gipp pointed to a battery of showers next his room-door.

"I'm the holy one around here," he said. "Cleanliness is always next to godliness."

This hallmark of humor which developed in what might be called his manners, step by step with the development of his athletic prowess, first stamped him — at least in my sight — as the solid-gold article called greatness. He displayed it first on the gridiron during the opening game of the 1919 season. This was against Kalamazoo, a medium-strong team.

Not desiring to pile up a score against Kalamazoo, and urgently wishing to give Gipp and the rest of the boys a strict test, with strict officials, I asked the officials to impose penalties without hesitation. Gipp shone in the first period with an 80-yard run. As the stands cheered the star's first touchdown of the season, the grim officials called back the ball, ruling one of our linemen offside. Within ten minutes Gipp broke through the entire Kalamazoo defense for a 68-yard run to a touchdown. Once more a grim field judge ruled a guard offside.

Gipp was mad clear through. He said nothing. Even during the intermission he made no bleat to me. That was one more striking piece of evidence that the boy had real, unmistakable class.

During the third period he hung back for a while, as we were ahead and it was always his whim to loaf when an opposing team was obviously weaker. But he caught a punt and couldn't resist the temptation to show his stuff as the crowd yelled: "Gipp! Gipp!" He tore off 70 yards and another touchdown. But the judge's whistle had blown just before Gipp crossed the line. Another penalty for holding.

Gipp strode by the official and quietly remarked:

"Next time give me one whistle to stop and two to keep

going."

This humor of his on the gridiron was rare, but good, and principally visible when our opponents were weak. On Thanksgiving Day in 1919, we had to meet Morningside College in Sioux City, Iowa. Five days before we had met and defeated Purdue in amiable weather. When we reached Sioux City it was 10 degrees above zero — so utterly cold that the Morningside players all wore white gloves at the beginning of the game. By the strangest coincidence, the Notre Dame line wore the white gloves after the third play. I don't know how it happened, but I distinctly remember that when Cy DeGree, a punctilious Notre Dame tackle, was called back to punt, he stripped off his gloves and passed them to the referee — Quigley, famous National League Baseball Umpire — saying, "Please hold these for me while I kick."

Gipp would not work on that day.

"It's too damned cold," he told me when I urged him to show the spectators some of his speed. The field was iron hard with zero cold and reduced our playing superiority over Morningside so much that after long battling we could score only two touchdowns. Gipp came over to the sidelines and said, "It's too cold. Take me out."

"One more touchdown," I said.

Back went word that the team must have another touchdown, just one more. Gipp was passed the ball on his 17-yard line. Viciously he ripped through the Morningside players. I pitied them because he looked mad. Breaking clear, he bowled over the secondaries one after another and tore down the field for 80 yards before his cleats slipped and a speedy opponent helped pin him down. On the next play we fumbled. Gipp turned to where I sat crouched at the sideline, pointed to the Morningside player hugging the ball and shrugged his shoulders eloquently.

Some native principle of conserving energy fashioned his conduct against weak teams. In an important game he never wavered, never flinched; he was striking energy every second. For a star (and before he had gone very far in 1919 the word that flew around the grandstands was "Gipp! Gipp!") he had no temperament and certainly no tremors. He never spared himself. He'd take out an end for any other ball carrier even more quickly than they'd cut the man down for him. Gipp never hesitated, never held himself precious. Only against pushovers was he lazy and deliberate, reducing his effort to a minimum when an easy game was on ice.

The high dramatic moments of the major battles found him daring, hard-hitting, almost vicious in his attack. What made him a marvel was that no matter how feverishly eager he appeared, he was always internally cool.

In the Army game of 1919, the Cadets had us at a disadvantage of 9 to 0 — and it looked as if they were going to hold it. Toward the end of the first half the Notre Dame quarterback, Joe Brandy, opened up a passing attack — Gipp throwing. This attack culminated with a cannonball pass from Gipp to Pete Bahan on the Army's 1-yard line. The teams lined up, Ojay Larson, at center for us, awaited signals when Gipp called sharply:

"Pass me the ball!"

Gipp had had a flash of the head linesman lifting his horn to blow the end of the half. While both teams looked on in surprise he grabbed the ball from Larson and dove over the goal line for a touchdown. The instant Gipp caught the ball the linesman's horn sounded; but the half wasn't over until the ball was dead, and the ball wasn't dead until the touchdown was made. I've never seen a quicker piece of thinking on the part of a player.

Nor have I ever seen a better balance of versatility — of slow acting as the result of quick thinking — than in perhaps the most grueling game Notre Dame ever played with its toughest western opponent, Nebraska. This was in 1919. In the opening scrimmage that season we had seven men badly hurt, but they got well enough to go with the squad to Lincoln.

Before 10 seconds of the game had passed, Gipp, going behind a phalanx of Nebraska players, flipped the ball to Dutch Bergman just as he'd flip a cigarette. Bergman, a clear field ahead, ran for a touchdown. War was declared and that game became grim and bruising. Nebraska scored. We went into the second half with a one-point edge, as they had failed at goal. We scored again. But the battering our men were getting had its effect. All available Notre Dame subs were used up by the beginning of the final period. The Nebraska bench was loaded with fresh players, eager to get in.

The Cornhuskers realized they had us on the run, although we led by 14 to 6. They came on stronger than ever as the fourth period opened; threw us back and kicked a goal for three points. The score was 14 to 9, 12 minutes to go and the Notre Dame men were dragging their legs, worn out, and no replacements.

Gipp took command, and the ball.

"Let's stall," he told his quarterback. So they stood talking while the watch ran on. A minute was killed. The referee came up, penalized us 5 yards.

"Why," said Gipp in indignant surprise, "I thought time was out."

"Think again," said the referee.

In subsequent plays when the rest of the backfield shifted one way Gipp would shift the other, and they'd have to do it all over again — all the while the watch was running, eating up seconds. Cautioned about that, Gipp pulled another trick. Carrying the ball, he'd let himself be tackled and when he went down he held the other players in a hug and shouted, "Let me up!"

He took 15 to 20 seconds before he'd let them let him up. The crowd roared impatiently; the players chafed, seeing precious minutes eaten up by dilatory tactics. Gipp tantalized them by kicking the ball cleverly out of bounds; he urged our quarterback to stutter signals and make them last longer. In brief, he killed minute after minute until the whistle blew and we won.

Nebraska's chagrined coach, good old Henry Schulte, said to Gipp, "What course do you take at Notre Dame?"

"Plumbing," laughed Gipp.

Gipp delighted in improvising strategy. Nebraska had tasted that before in 1918 when our first- and second-string quarterbacks were hurt and the third quarterback was knocked out. Gipp switched to the quarterback position and shouted signals with glorious abandon. He alternated energy with leisureliness. Against Purdue in 1919, on the first play of the second quarter, he ran 90 yards for a touchdown. Content with that burst of energy he was called on to run again, but said, so that the Purdue men could hear, "Oh, no. Let's pass."

And he passed them dizzy.

Before I forget the Nebraska game in 1918! Gipp took a fancy that another player should make the touchdown. He gave him the ball and the line opened holes. But Nebraska stiffened and was holding us. Gipp passed word to the other halfback to follow him on a line plunge at Nebraska's 10-yard mark. Gipp carried the player hanging on to his belt across the goal line, but a keen field judge disallowed the score and penalized Notre Dame 15-yards. He had seen the player towed by Gipp's belt.

In game after game Gipp showed the same resourcefulness. Sometimes it succeeded, less often it failed. But his ingenuity and initiative never failed. Nor did his courage. Against Indiana in the game of 1920, which I have mentioned before, we were a beaten team. We thought it would be an easy win. It wasn't. Gipp's shoulder was dislocated. I took him out. The Hoosiers led us 10-0 and the game had only minutes to go. The ball went down in a fury of old Notre Dame fighting spirit to Indiana's 7-yard line. The third quarter ended and, by the rules, I could substitute any one I wanted. Gipp, the cripple, came to me and insisted upon going in. Reluctantly, I consented.

He charged on the field, and the stands rose to acclaim.

Rarely have I seen a more thrilling sight than those stands, gaunt in dusk, banked thousands screaming the name of one man — Gipp!

Of course he was marked. The Indiana men, their first victory over us in 30 years smelling sweet in their nostrils, weren't going to let a crippled hero beat them. But the crippled hero had something to say about that. He tried once — disdaining runs, passing. With a smashed shoulder he smashed the line — and failed.

Indiana roared.

He tried again. Taking the ball, he crouched into a self-driven battering ram. Smash — and over he went!

But I'm stressing too much the picturesque and dramatic offensive plays that brought George Gipp into the limelight — in which he knew how to comport himself without the slightest increase in self-esteem, or the remotest hint of condescension toward humbler members of the combination on which he played. Gipp was a master of defense as well. And I can say of him what cannot, I believe, be said of any other football player, certainly not of any other Notre Dame player — that not a single forward pass was ever completed in territory defended by George Gipp. He had the timing of a tiger in pouncing on its prey. He never missed.

A great player — what everybody who knew him in and out of school called "a great guy" — Gipp had a weakness. Before I learned at firsthand what it was I had seen a striking exhibition of it in a football game. Those who saw the Army-Notre Dame game in 1920 may remember that at a point when the Army led us by 17 to 14 near the end of the first half, Gipp did a strange thing. The quarterback called for a kick, and our men set in motion for formation. Gipp was to kick, and the position sent him behind his own goal line. As even a neophyte knows, when behind your own goal line there is only one orthodox thing to do — and that is kick. The Army, a citadel of orthodox football, knew the kick was coming, and they were pressing to receive it to keep their score ahead of Notre Dame's.

But Gipp was not orthodox. Passing another player, Roger Kiley, on his way to receive the ball he warned him, "When I get the ball tear ahead. I'll pass it."

Gipp took the snap-back, poised to kick. Army charged. Before a finger could touch him he had sidestepped and thrown the ball 45 yards to Kiley in a field as free as the ocean. But Kiley, for the first and only time in his career, dropped the ball.

That was gambling — absolute gambling. Gipp made amends — for a mistake he hadn't committed — by ripping the Army line to pieces in the second half and putting his team in front for the final count of 27-17, but he had proved to me that he was a gambler.

I learned later, after his death, that this was so. I had often wondered why George Gipp, not a rich boy, had always sufficient funds. He was an expert card-player, an expert billiards-player — expert as he would have been in almost anything he took up. It was his pastime to go to rendezvous of visiting gentlemen of the trade and beat them at their own games.

Superficially it never affected his training, for his physical condition seemed splendid always. He could sprint a hundred yards in 10 and one-fifth seconds any and every day. But on a damp freezing afternoon he contracted an infected sore throat. The whole city of South Bend joined the crowded university in anxiety over Gipp. It was touching to go through the streets and have utter strangers stop me and ask, "How is he? Any change?"

The lad never knew how personally popular he was among and above a popular team. When Grantland Rice and other prominent sportswriters went for the first time to West Point to report an Army-Notre Dame game and to view this wonder-man Gipp, their staccato praise the next day meant little to him. An ordinarily self-appreciative player would have bought every newspaper in sight and read the clippings until he'd memorized them backward. Gipp didn't even read them once! So far as I'm aware he never posed for a photograph. The only photo I have of him is one snapped on the playing field.

It became national news when George Gipp died. But that was only the measure of his athletic celebrity.

What was never in the news was his utter gameness.

I bent over this boy of 25 — who had scaled the glamourous heights of all boyhood dreams by shining as a national football hero. The Chicago Cubs had just bid for his baseball services on graduation. Walter Camp had just named him all-America fullback.

"It's pretty tough to go," said someone at the bedside.

"What's tough about it?" Gipp smiled up at us feebly. "I've no complaint."

He turned to me.

"I've got to go, Rock," he said. "It's all right. I'm not afraid." His eyes brightened in a frame of pallor. "Some time, Rock," he said, "when the team's up against it; when things are wrong and the breaks are beating the boys — tell them to go in there with all they've got and win just one for the Gipper. I don't know where I'll be then, Rock. But I'll know about it, and I'll be happy."

In 1928, the team had a tough season — a punishing season — cracked by Wisconsin in its second game, licked by Georgia Tech. All but demoralized. Then came the Army — Gipp's old love and hate. The cadets had spread ruin almost everywhere that year. And they were out to give Notre Dame the beating of years. At the half we were even, nothing to nothing.

For the first time since Gipp's death I told the boys what he had said. These lads on that 1928 team had never met Gipp — had never seen him. But Gipp is a legend at Notre Dame. Every football writer at that halftime said that Notre Dame would be beaten badly. It looked as if we were weakening. But the boys came out for the second half exalted, inspired, overpowering.

They won.

As Chevigny slashed through for the first touchdown he said, "That's one for the Gipper!"

A boy does well indeed who, so young, leaves the clean glory of a name behind.

May his soul rest in peace!

TO SHIFT OR NOT TO SHIFT

Theodore Roosevelt, apostle and exemplar of the strenuous life, decided one day that football was far too strenuous. There was popular hue and cry against a game that resulted in scores and even hundreds of casualties every year. President Roosevelt summoned to a White House conference representatives of the then truly called Big Three — Yale, Harvard and Princeton — and urged upon them the necessity of saving football from public disfavor by revising the rules to give brain a chance over brawn.

When somebody at the conference chided the President that as he personally lived a strenuous life he should let football players do likewise without interference, Roosevelt made a characteristic reply, "These players are boys who must be protected against the natural recklessness of youth. I believe the game can be made more interesting and less brutal without in any way impairing its manliness."

The President was right; but a search of football annals does not show that his sound judgment was instantly recognized. The savage, battering-ram style of play went on — probably because that was all the coaches knew or cared to teach their players. Turtleback, guardback and tackle-back plays, with their solid smash and impact that always meant bruised bodies and often broken bones, went on for a while as if the President had not intervened. My memory goes back to games witnessed at that time and they resembled very much what we now call a battle royal — where assorted gentlemen in a ring try to disassemble one another as completely and as expeditiously as possible.

As an example of how rough the game was in those days, and how closely line play approached assault and battery, I repeat a story told by an old-timer who bragged recently to a group of coaches about the good old he-man days of that period. This chap, who is now a prominent business man, was lamenting what he called the cream-puff type of football being played today, "In my time," he said, "those were the days when men were men. I remember distinctly what Spartan fortitude was required of us in those halcyon days. Then the game was a game and rules were secondary, sometimes not even that.

"I played in a game once that stands out in memory as typical of the real old football. We were playing a certain college in the East. We had a line coach whom we'll call Lowbrow. He had spent much time and a vast vocabulary teaching us the fine points of center play. A favorite trick of his on defense was to have the defensive center knee the offensive center passing the ball just at the moment when the offensive center was most helpless to protect himself. Lowbrow spent hours teaching us this little trick. In this particular game, all during the first half I was making tackles all over the field and doing what I thought was a yeoman job.

"As we came in between halves, however, instead of the compliments which I'd been expecting, Lowbrow came to me and said, "You didn't do it! You didn't do it!"

" 'Didn't do what?' I said.

" 'You didn't knee him,' he said, and added, 'I want that done in the first play in the second half.'

"So, in the second half, our opponents received the kick, and on the first play I kneed the opposing center with skillful technique, laying him out like a rug.

"A deft bit of art, but it started the fireworks. On the following play the whole opposing line converged on me, knocked me down and played hopscotch on my anatomy. I believe as a result of this individual attention from the reception committee, that I was inspired to introduce the role now known as roving center. It was a matter of interest, because for the next play I dropped back six or seven yards where I could see the player who was coming at me, after which I roved rapidly in another direction.

"Our opponents had a remarkable halfback named Gilroy. I received sudden information from the coach on the bench that Gilroy must be eliminated. So the next time Gilroy carried the ball I dove into him, and Gilroy was just blotted out, as they put it figuratively. That hazard was removed. Our opponents then began using a huge chap named Casey on a tackle-back play, which was most effective, as our little right end, weighing 140 pounds, could hardly annoy this mastodon.

"On receiving instructions I moved out in Casey's vicinity, and when he charged through carrying the ball I wrapped my arm around his neck, intending to throw him back where he came from. To my consternation he began biting at my biceps as though he were eating corn on the cob.

"I protested vociferously and, reinforced by my captain, we carried the protest to the referee with much gusto. The referee was very much perplexed — saying he had not seen anything — but he finally said when we demanded he do something about it, " 'I suggest that next year, when you play these boys, you play them on Friday.' "

This old-timer's story is probably an exaggeration of what really happened. But there's no question that in those push-and-pull, mass-and-tackle plays, there was much rough stuff that added nothing to the game and that could well be eliminated — and with the hue and cry gathering momentum something had to be done. Hence the alert intervention by President Roosevelt.

The spirit animating many players of those days is well illustrated by the story of the coach who conceived the idea that
during the warm month of September, the thing to do with his
football squad was not to practice the hard driving game as we
know it, but to play soccer instead. This could be done in track
suits instead of heavy football uniforms — and soccer was a
great conditioner, as it involved a lot of running. So the coach
went down to the local sporting goods store and bought a soccer
ball which he brought out to his squad. He told the boys what he
had in mind.

"Now," he said, "I haven't got time to go into the difference
in rules between soccer and the American game of football. So
this afternoon, for simplicity's sake, we'll just bear two things in
mind. Either kick the ball or kick your opponent on the shins."

Having divided his squad into equal sides the coach looked
around vainly for the new soccer ball.

"Where the deuce is that ball I bought this afternoon?" he
asked.

A new candidate for football honors, an enthusiastic young
Celt, cried out, "To heck with the ball. Let's start the game."

That original and actual version of a twice-told tale illustrates
the old spirit which necessitated new rules.

An old friend of mine who has never missed seeing a football
game between two major schools every Saturday in the season,
summarized the difference between the game according to the
old, sock-'em and rock-'em rules, with the new, open and artistic game.

"I remember seeing Indiana play Illinois," he said one
November day. "It was dusky and sleety, and that may have impaired my vision. But I was young then and an alert spectator.
Yet I kept count of the number of times I saw the ball in play —
five exactly.

"Last season I compared notes with this game of twenty years ago and actually lost count of the times I saw the ball in play. The old game was man against man — in which game a tug of war would be a better gauge of superior power. The new game is still man against man — but for the ball. The football has at last achieved the place it should have in the game of football.''

In the middle of the nineteenth century, it was, that freshmen at such schools as Harvard, Princeton and Rutgers were informally kicking around an inflated pig's bladder, playing an impromptu game having few or no rules. Interest in this game developed, and as it grew it became necessary to have definite rules, particularly when a group of students in one school informally challenged a similar group from another.

Up until 1876, Yale, Princeton, Harvard and Rutgers had played a few contests, using in some cases a modification of the association game, and in other cases a modification of English rugby. These same schools met with Columbia in a convention at Springfield, Massachusetts, in 1876, where American football was born by introducing two distinct departures from the English game of rugby. The first of these was that the center should pass the ball to a quarterback who, in turn, could pass it to any one of his players behind him — which differed considerably from the rather indiscriminate *scrum* known in rugby. In that English game the score was computed by field goals. At the Springfield meeting, the Americans changed the rules so as to make four touchdowns equal to a field goal. This was the start of the game as we know it today.

The great Walter Camp, who did more for American football than any other individual, was on the Yale team that fall, and for 40 years thereafter he was largely responsible for the evolution of the game to its present form.

This informal rules committee, which began functioning in 1876, continued to do so up until 1899, when there was a severe rupture. Two football tribunals appeared on the scene: one composed of Navy, Princeton and Yale; the other of Cornell, Har-

vard and Pennsylvania. Previous to this time, the rules committee, while not representative of the whole country, made rules
for the rest of the schools, and these rules were accepted around
the country through recognition of the merit and labor of the
committee.

Followers of the game — not many in those days — had seen
certain features of football come and go, such as the murderous
flying wedge of De Land of Harvard and all the other attendant
rough phases of the game. Divided authority brought chaos into
the administration of rules for the game until Walter Camp
stepped into the breach and by tact and judgment reconciled the
two rulemaking bodies, which merged into one committee,
which, in turn, functioned smoothly until 1905.

But while the six rules functioned smoothly — that is, without
divided authority in legislating for football — the game was exceedingly rough under those rules. Examine the records
available and you'll find that heavier teams invariably defeated
lighter teams and certainly that the lighter teams suffered much
larger casualties. The hard drive, without recourse to deceptive
tactics in and back of the line — except tricks of an elementary
kind like the hidden ball — gave the bull-necked boys a
devastating edge over smaller if brainier opponents. So the game
was a modified shambles, and outcry arose against it and
Roosevelt intervened.

The result was that Walter Camp, Amos Alonzo Stagg and
other leaders in the game tried to devise rules against roughness
— and did. But what the game needed was not rules that could
be violated with impunity in the rush and confusion of play, but
a new device in the game itself to make its playing less hazard-
ous.

To Stagg goes credit for this revolution in football that gave us
the shift — the dramatic equalizer between "big" teams and
"little" teams.

The shift quickly became popular. It was new and spectacular and gave the untechnical football fan a chance to see something of the game besides mass huddles, flying wedges and stretcher-bearers. Likewise it stimulated coaches to real thought for they had to devise defenses to meet the shift and variations of the shift to penetrate old-time defenses.

And now we find, after 25 years of the shift, in which period it has been developed to marvelous precision, a definite movement to cripple or abolish it. Frankly, I can't understand why.

Perhaps when Jim Corbett introduced clever boxing and footwork against John L. Sullivan down in New Orleans in 1892, the old diehards of that day felt just as bitter because Jim danced in and hit Sullivan before Sullivan could hit back — for Jim, by that time, was shifting nimbly and safely away.

Stagg at Chicago and Williams at Minnesota, the great masters of the evolutions and gyrations of the shift, are pioneers in football who have not even been consulted by those who would abolish it.

The shift and the forward pass have done much to popularize football. About a third of the teams in the country, high schools and colleges, use the shift in some form or other. Football fans from coast to coast love to watch it. Evidently they realize that, without the shift, the game would often become dull and monotonous. Boys who have played football on teams using the shift attack never can or will go back to the "set and wait" method of advancing the ball. This used to be called set and go, but set and wait is better. That's exactly what many teams do.

The shift has the lilt and the nuance of the Hungarian gypsy, plus the verve and élan of the Cossack and the rhythm of the Chester Hale girls. It has augmented the pageantry of the game and has become an integral part of football.

Its best technical advantage is that it gives the small man, the clever chap, the quick-mover and quick-thinker, a chance to play the game on equal terms with the big bruising fellow. To abolish either the shift or the forward pass would be reactionary in the extreme and not in the best interest of the public, which enjoys the game, or of the players, who enjoy playing it as it is.

In 1929, the rules committee changed the shift rule — for reasons no one can fathom. At the Football Coaches' Association annual meeting in December 1929, when the rules were discussed, the shift was not even mentioned. Neither was the shift discussed at the two previous meetings of the rules committee which I attended. Apparently everything was going smoothly.

Let me mention that shifting teams stopped completely and lost momentum under the old rule which stipulated that they must stop for approximately one second. Yet the new rule states that the shifting team must stop for at least one second, after shifting into position, with the suggestion that this passage of time be measured by the referee counting up to six. Now, no shifting coach objects to his team stopping at least one second; but the only way we can measure one second is by a stop watch. Who can measure time uniformly by counting? The rule might just as well say that 36 inches can be measured by stating that it is a yard, or by saying that it is three times the length of an official's shoe. In which case the question of variation arises — as is does in speed of count. An official like John Schommer has unusually small feet, but there are officials of the Primo Carnera type — and who shall say what feet like those of the vest-pocket Venetian will measure when laid end to end?

As an example of the effect this rule, requiring that an official count to six after the shift, has had on the minds of some football coaches, I quote a letter from a coach in a small college in the East:

"The split infinitive has always been the amusing bane of English classes; but it will be as nothing compared to the absurdity of split-second timing which we in the East will be up against if any of us tries to use the shift this fall. Whether or not there is any momentum lost, or unfair advantage, will not be considered. We have several officials who stutter as badly as old Tiny Maxwell used to. By the time they count to six, two or three seconds will be consumed, and the effect of the shift will have been lost no matter how stupid the opposition.

"So I'm going to change my style of attack, and likewise the style of my material. Enclosed is a snapshot which shows my last year's team. What do you think of this smart-looking bunch of boys? Neat, trim ankles — and all that. But this is all past. The material I want for next fall is not the alert, aggressive type, but the cow-minded, hippopotamus-chassised type. I'll send you a picture of the new crowd, and you'll notice their bovine expressions and how ox-knuckle ankles predominate. One man in the picture will be wearing a mustache and doing the best he can to exude an aroma of strategic cunning. That will be me.

"What do you intend to do?"

The question is what lawyers call a leading one. I never could wear a mustache — but I might try a beard!

Seriously, to meet the new rule our team will be drilled so that after the shift, they will stop for one and two-tenths seconds, making sure to stop completely and lose momentum. And that is all anybody can ask in fairness.

Personally, I don't care what style of football our opponents use. When Notre Dame played Rutgers some years ago, Foster Sanford complained about our backs being in motion too soon. The game had been gaily vigorous. Some of my backs had not only been in motion, but in commotion. They had been carried from the field. So that when Sanford reiterated his demand, saying, "I insist that Rockne's backs remain rigid," all I could reply was, "That's the trouble. Four or five of my backs are rigid now — but thank Heaven I've got enough good substitutes to see the game through."

To me it is amusing that the rules committee meeting, despite

157

the fact that one-third of the colleges of the country are using the shift — did not hear what these colleges might want to say about it, for they were not represented in any shape, manner or form on the rules committee or on any advisory committee. If my history is correct, the American Revolutionary War was distinguished for a slogan that said something about "taxation without representation." I believe the coaches who use the shift have today a similar grievance. We are experiencing legislation without true representation.

Many of the coaches who now object to the shift tried to play it once themselves, but not with conspicuous success. The matter of timing, rhythm and counting is complicated, but not difficult when fully grasped. The shift provides the advantage of deployment — of catching an opponent out of position and off balance which the quick shift makes possible.

Football is not or should not be merely a game for the strong and stupid. It should be a game for the smart, the swift, the brave and the clever boy. The Four Horsemen could never have played football under the old rules without the shift. These four lads averaged 158 pounds in weight, and the qualities that made them remarkable were not bruising strength or crushing power, or irresistible momentum — but brains, speed, cleverness, finesse and superb strategy.

The leading schools from the point of view of impressive records last year were the University of Southern California and St. Mary's on the Pacific Coast; Purdue and Notre Dame in the Middle West; Tulane and Florida in the South; with New York University in the East. All were shifting teams.

Personally, I have unbounded faith in the fairness and judgment of my good friend, Mr. E. K. Hall, chairman of the rules committee, but were the shifting coaches permitted to have one representative to present their viewpoint, I believe the shift would be allowed to remain an integral part of football. If it goes much of the spectacle of football will go with it — and the battering, bruising game may yet return to put beef at a premium and brains at a discount.

Or perhaps a shifting team will be driven to the necessity, when the officials are timing the shift, to time the timers. It complicates rules already somewhat difficult for the public, which supports the game, to understand fully.

One thing stands out in my football experience — that the officials appointed to enforce the rules are almost invariably fair. I've seen cases where officials have erred, mistakes of judgment, and rarer cases where they have erred in their knowledge of the rules. But in all my years I have known of but one case where an official was prejudiced and unfair. In this game Notre Dame thought the official was somewhat biased. We knew it, when both teams were near the sideline and there came a fumble. First our opponents had possession, then Notre Dame took possession, after which the ball went out of bounds. Our captain came quickly forward and shouted to the referee, "Notre Dame's ball! Notre Dame's ball!"

The referee strode forward belligerently and said, "No, no! *Our* ball!"

Officials are human and prone to error in applying the rules, and if everybody objected to close decisions that were adverse the game would collapse and collegiate contests would become pandemonium with referees and field judges being chased far and wide through the not so stilly night. But outlawing the shift is a threat against the game, and imposing a long, Tunney-Dempsey count on the shift is one way to oulaw it.

A prominent coach who objects to the shift draws this analogy: the shifting team, he says, has the same advantage over a non-shifting team which the footrunner with a flying start has over the footrunner who uses the standard start. This is unfair, when both runners can — if they will — start in the same way. The shift in football is analogous to the flank movement in warfare, so successfully employed by Frederick the Great,

Napoleon and other master generals.

In football, on an end run, the men on the line of an offensive team are the infantrymen, the backfield interference the light artillery. On a line plunge, the line becomes the artillery barrage and shock troops to open up a hole and the backfield becomes the infantry to pour through. The quarterback is the chief of staff. Changing the method of attack, sending a man back to punt, is similar to a change in pitching the battlefield. On the forward pass play, the backfield and the ends become an airplane squadron, and if the pass is successful, it is analogous to destroying a supply depot or the base of communications of the defensive team.

Now, as regards the defensive team against an end run the line is the infantry, while the defensive ends are machine-gunners who pepper the advancing interference in its attempts to try to get the man with the ball. The backfield is the mobile cavalry moving to support the attack point.

Against a line plunge the defensive line is artillerymen who try to break it up before it gets under way.

Against a forward pass the line is heavy artillery who try to pepper the hangars of the aerial squadron while the backfield men change from cavalry into anti-aircraft guns or to airplane squadrons in their attempts to frustrate the completion of the forward pass. The commanders-in-chief are the coaches on the sidelines, the water boy is the commissary, and the alumni of both opposing schools sit in the stands as Congress and pass judgment on the commanders-in-chief and their strategy.

Or football can be said to be a glorified game of chess, with the players as pawns and the quarterbacks as movers of the men, who must think as any chess player thinks, but more quickly as not more than 30 seconds is allowed for the calling of each play.

Any game in which 22 men play could be much more complex, but the rules committee has worked well in keeping the game as simple as possible, which is why undue complexity such as in the count of six at the shift militates against making the game and its finer points easily understandable.

If complexity is desired it would be easy to put the game on a plane of the Chinese puzzle. For instance, the peculiarities and eccentricities of individuals and teams might be put to scrutiny, and, if they failed to measure up to standards, penalties be inflicted even before a game begins. Every group of football players has its whims and weaknesses. We of Notre Dame used to have the superstition at Lincoln, Nebraska, that if we walked backward into the stadium, we'd win. As a matter of fact we won twice running by this backward walk, or so we thought. Until, a third time, with due ceremony we entered the stadium face last and were hopelessly squelched. The superstition was squelched with us.

I personally originated a superstition, shared by the team, about a flute I used to play. Indeed, it was said of me that I could make a better run on a flute than any other left end in the country. Once, when we were en route for a game away from home, on opening my bag the flute was missing. The entire squad chased me back home for the magic flute — which apparently had lost its magic, for we were beaten.

Rules of the game can make it or ruin it. It would be possible to bring up rule after rule and show how it might be improved. As things stand, however, we have a workable code, even if it's elaborate. The bane of coaches, officials and rules committees is freaks with legal or legalistic minds — not one and the same thing, but many and different — who propound hypothetical questions seeking to add new rules as if there were not enough. All the rules, as written, cover every conceivable circumstance or "break" in the game. This does not prevent the pundits from putting such luscious problems as, for instance, this:

Harvard has time out and the water boy is out with the water bucket. Two minutes' time allowed is up, and the referee blows his whistle that play must resume. The teams line up, with Harvard in punt formation, Yale on defense. The water boy is slow leaving the field. Before he is off the field the Harvard center snaps the ball back to the kicker and the kick goes to one side, the ball lands in the water bucket and the water boy carries it off the field. What is the rule?

Here's another example of a similar type of question:

Stanford is playing California. They have reached California's 40-yard line with the fourth down, and they elect to take place-kick formation. The Stanford center snaps the ball and Stanford's quarterback places the ball on the ground for his kicker. The Stanford kicker, however, can't reach the ball before a California guard has broken through and run full-tilt into the ball, causing the ball to go in the opposite direction and, lo and behold, it goes between the goalposts.

Here's another question:

Michigan is playing Illinois. The Michigan team takes punt formation and their punter punts 50 yards down the field to the Illinois quarterback. The Illinois quarterback catches the ball, but instead of running with it kicks it back 50 yards where it is caught by the Michigan kicker who hasn't moved an inch. The Michigan kicker now, instead of kicking back, throws a long forward pass down the field to one of his ends.

These hypothetical questions can all be answered satisfactorily by an official who knows the rules thoroughly. But the average spectator should not worry about hypothetical questions of this kind because they can not happen. So enjoy the game and don't worry about technical quibbling over matters which should be debated only by philosophers or professors of education.

But since the codified and voluminous rules satisfy everybody — with one exception — this new shift rule that's agitating the football world should be explained wherein the rule is fair to shifting coaches.

When a lineman on the offensive team is offside, the penalty is 5 yards, provided the offensive team is not a shifting team. If a lineman on the shifting team is offside, the penalty is 15 yards, even though the lineman has taken no part in the shift and hasn't moved. This is just merely a sample of the class legislation which the teams using the shift are up against.

Personally, I think the coaches in the East ought to get together and have something to say about football as they used to in the days of Percy Haughton, Charlie Daly, Dave Fallwell and Tad Jones. In those days, the graduate manager used to see that the grass on the field was cut, the field marked, the football suits taken out of the moth balls. He also arranged the schedule. Today, in conjunction with some haberdashers, insurance salesmen and brokerage clerks, these graduate managers interpret the rules, pick the officials, hire and fire the coaches.

If the shift is abolished in football, I believe the game will lose its present popularity, interest and color both for the player and spectator. Everybody will be a punt player or a double wing back and the game will become standardized and monotonous.

Some coaches lost their offense two years ago when the fumble rule was introduced. Last year their offense consisted of two long passes, a prayer and a punt. When they saw the success of the Warner system and the shift system, they immediately turned against the shift. They will probably turn against the Warner system next by making it illegal to have wing backs. They will simplify matters and ten years from now the annual contest between Yale and Princeton will be a tug of war so as to eliminate the equipment and to keep the contest one to determine which school has the most physical power, a simple one. It might not be a bad thing for the Coaches' Association at the next meeting to insist that the rules be left unchanged for five years and tell all the impedimenta such as commissioners and officials themselves and others that the game is to be left as it is for this period and changed for no reason. I know the coaches I have talked to think this would be good for the game technically and popularly.

THE GAME THAT THRILLS

I was surprised one afternoon by the appearance in my office of a young man with a mild reputation for intellect. He had taken exception to remarks I had made at a football mass meeting. He believed, and stated emphatically, that culture had little place in schools where football was the major athletic interest. We entered into friendly debate — on this much misunderstood question of culture. He gave me his definition, which I cannot hope to repeat as my vocabulary is limited. Then I gave him mine.

I was riding, I told him, on the Blue Train from the Riviera to Paris. Sharing a compartment with me was a dapper little Frenchman, neatly turned out, with boulevard clothes and hair shinily docile under heavy layers of pomade, which had also been applied to what might be termed a circumflex-accent mustache.

In the morning, I arose, while my companion slept soundly. Opening my bag I searched for soap — as there seems to be a European prejudice against supplying soap to travelers. I had exported a good supply. Stripping to the waist I gave myself the benefit of copious suds and water, and emerged, shining with cleanliness.

The splashing awakened my companion. He also got up and with the few words we had in common, plus appropriate gestures, indicated he'd like to eat breakfast with me.

I assented, and waited for him to complete his toilet. As I had looked into my bag for soap, he looked into his. But, instead of soap, he brought out a perfume spray, sprinkled his face delicately — that was all — and — presto! (as I said to my young friend) he was finished. I went out to breakfast glowing with a brash, rough, American soap-and-water scrubbing. My little foreign friend went out covered with culture.

Football and all athletics should be a part of culture, the culture that makes the whole man, not the part-time thinker. Ancient Greece was a cradle of culture, and ancient Greece was a nation of athletes. In Europe, or those parts of it where football and athletics are unknown, the place of healthy, skillful, physical play is taken by none too wholesome dueling and promotion of a warlike spirit that may be virile, but is anything but cultural.

Boys must have an outlet for animal spirits. Their education must contain a training in clean contests, otherwise they'll be lost in a world that thrives on competition and in which those who cannot compete cannot hope to thrive.

Football, as the leading American amateur pastime, provides participants, students and other spectators with the most colorful, the most skillful and the most beneficial of all athletic contests: which is why it stirs the pulse, captures the imagination and, at the same time, builds character without which culture is valueless.

Looking back over my career in football — not a long career, but, if I'm permitted to say so, typical of the average American coach — it's studded with the thrills that ensue from the drama of the gridiron to exhilarate onlookers and give to the young and their elders the something heroic in times of peace that stirs men quite as much, and to quite as important a cultural purpose, as the heroics of war.

The first big thrill that came to me in football was when I saw Chicago beat Michigan on Thanksgiving Day 1905. The only score made was by Chicago, which won 2-0, and that came when Catlin, the Chicago end, threw a Michigan back over the goal line for a safety. That is, it was a safety in those days: under the present rules it would not have been. However, this was not the highlight of the game to me. It was my old hero, Walter Eckersall, who caused the chills to run up and down my spine, and whose remarkably daring play lives in my memory as heroism in action.

Chicago had the ball on third down and Eckersall was dropped back to kick. So close was the ball to his own goal line that Eckersall lined up behind it. The Michigan team concentrated to block him. Michigan had been pressing Chicago hard, and the spectators sensed that a break was imminent. A strong wind blew against Eckersall. Everyone, including the Michigan team, figured he could do nothing but kick. Back went the ball to Eckersall. He made a slight move as if to kick, and then he went streaking around left end, circling the rushing Michigan end who could not change his course. On up the field Eckersall went 35 yards — to safety as far as the Chicago team was concerned, for his next kick landed deep in Michigan territory. What would have happened had Eckersall been downed for a safety I hate to think of. But why think of it? Here was daring, imagination, steely nerve and immediate execution.

I had a thrill of another kind in those early days when our North West Division high school team scrimmaged informally with the great North Division team in Chicago. Included in the North Division personnel was Walter Steffen, today a judge in Chicago and coach of Carnegie Tech. If there was one thing I ever prided myself on it was my ability to tackle. At least 20 times that afternoon I left my feet with all the length I could muster and with arms outstretched catapulted myself at Steffen who was carrying the ball. But it was just a dive into space with a dull thud as my body struck the ground. Steffen was there and he wasn't there. After the game was over and I limped, bruised, to the sideline, Steffen came up, slapped my back and said, "Nice tackling, boy. I had to step to keep out of your way."

Several years later, in a game I happened to attend, I saw this same Steffen who had become one of the greatest quarterbacks and field generals under Stagg of Chicago. In this game he was stopped dead by as great a pair of ends as ever played together on a football team. I refer to the fierce Sioux and the cunning Arapahoe, Gardner and Exendine, who were playing for Pop Warner on Carlisle. What a delight it was to see these two men work! Their down-the-field play under Pete Hauser's punts was as fine as I've ever seen — a thing of beauty. It was so good in fact, that in the second half Stagg changed his tactics against Pete Hauser's kicking, and put three men on each of the ends to prevent the Indian pair going down to cover the kick. The wily Hauser was alert. The next time he kicked, he stood there with the ball for at least four seconds while in the meantime Gardner and Exendine had broken loose and streaked down the field with Chief Afraid-of-a-Bear and Lone Star, when Hauser proceeded deliberately to boot the ball his usual 60 yards.

It was in this game I saw Pete Hauser rise up behind center and mop his forehead with a sort of half-yawn. The mop was just half finished and the yawn half completed when back snapped the ball and through the line went Hauser for 8 yards. The Chicago line had relaxed when they saw Hauser yawning and wiping his forehead.

Bret Harte tells us about the dark ways and vain tricks of the heathen Chinese, but in football, laurels for cunning go to the Indians.

In the fall of 1914, when I was assistant coach to Jess Harper, our first big league game was with Yale. Faculty, student body, townspeople and team were confident that it was just a question of the score. We hadn't been beaten in three years and everybody, including myself, was suffering from a bad case of what we call fathead. That is, all except Jess Harper. Jess pleaded and stormed like a lone voice in the wilderness, but all in vain. "Absurd," everyone said. "This Notre Dame team can't be beaten!"

I sat on the sideline at New Haven that Saturday afternoon and saw a good Yale team captained by Bud Talbot, with a crack halfback named Harry LeGore leading the attack. They made Notre Dame look like a high school squad. They lateral-passed Notre Dame out of the park and knocked our ears down to the tune of 28 to 0 — the most valuable lesson Notre Dame ever had in football. It taught us never to be cocksure. Modern football at Notre Dame can be dated from that game, as we made vital use of every lesson we learned.

On the following Monday, Jess Harper put in Stagg's backfield shift with my idea of flexing or shuttling the ends, which was the beginning of what is known in football today as the Notre Dame system.

Of course, the obvious thrill in football is the long run with the herd of opponents in full cry. I saw the first real thriller of this kind when Notre Dame played the Army in November 1915. The great Army halfback Elmer Oliphant had just made a fair catch on his own 48-yard line. This allowed him the privilege of a free kick. With his quarterback holding the ball, Oliphant sent the ball straight and true for the goalposts. It looked as if it were surely going over when it suddenly dropped in a downward arc, struck the crossbar and bounded back in the field of play. This made it a touchback and the ball was brought out 20 yards and given to Notre Dame. Three inches higher and Oliphant's kick would have won the game for Army. On the next play, Dutch Bergman gained 18 yards, ran out of bounds, fell over a bench and was severely injured. It did not seem that he could continue. But Bergman, besides being a great halfback, had the most remarkable powers of recuperation I have ever seen. With 30 seconds left to play, Notre Dame's quarterback, Jimmy Phelan, now coach at the University of Washington, called for a forward pass and Stan Cofall flicked a 15-yard pass to Bergman who caught it, dodged a halfback and outran the safety to the goal line — a gain of nearly 80 yards! Rooters on both sides were flabbergasted and it was minutes, I know, before I realized exactly what I had witnessed. A useful back to have, a boy like Bergman, ready to break loose for a touchdown at any time. So, for that matter, was Oliphant, who ranks with the truly great in the game.

Another kind of gridiron thrill — the first of its kind that came to me — was the thrill of the coach, which the spectators can scarcely share because they are usually unaware of the circumstances that bring it about. In our 1921 game with Army, Coach Daly of Army registered objections to the Notre Dame shift. In the first half we made two touchdowns, using the protested shift, but long passes — not the shift — were responsible for the scores. Between halves Daly repeated emphatically his complaint about our shift. So forcefully that the referee, Ed Thorp, said to me, "What am I going to do, Rock?"

"I'll relieve you of embarrassment," I said. "For the rest of the game, Notre Dame will use no shift. We'll just use stationary punt formation."

We did. Result? Two more touchdowns. The Army was outrun and outpassed. Daly came to me after the game and apologized for his protest. That was fine sportsmanship. No less fine was the thrill I had as coach realizing that my team could deny itself a powerful weapon and still win.

In every department of the game the coach gets a kick out of fine play that the spectators often miss. Eight years ago, Georgia Tech, the Golden Tornado, had the famous Red Barron at halfback. Our whole problem was: Can we stop Barron? All week we drilled on tackling and it looked terrible. The more we drilled the worse it looked. Remember that an unofficial game in Carlinville had played havoc with both Notre Dame and the University of Illinois, as several players from both schools had stepped out to make an honest dollar in a pro game. They were, of course, dropped, and we were handicapped. Our men were green. Before the game I read a wire to the team from my little son, Bill, who was ill at the time. He telegraphed that he wanted his daddy's team to win quickly so that his daddy could come home early.

Those green boys, who had been so bad in practice, went out and put on an astonishing exhibition of tackling. They stopped the dreaded Red Barron with streaking charges. A blind man could have enjoyed those tackles. They sounded strong, hard and clean. Barron fumbled seven times when hit and we won 13 to 3. Tackling did it.

Sheer picturesqueness of play was never better illustrated than in two Notre Dame scoring plays in 1926 — Christie Flanagan against Army and Art Parisien against Southern California. In the Army game there never were two teams more evenly matched. As the first half drew to a close, it was evident to the expert eye that these two teams might play for days without a score. However, Harry O'Boyle, our fullback, was puncturing the line for short, sure gains, which was annoying them. John J. McEwen, the Army line coach, was using a unique defense to nullify the technique of the Notre Dame ends in blocking tackles. He dropped the Army tackles back three yards. This stopped Flanagan's wide runs, but it left them vulnerable to O'Boyle's plunges.

In the second half, Army kicked off. It became our ball on our 30-yard line. The first play was a plunge for no gain. But John Wallace, Notre Dame right end, told Edwards, the quarterback, in a huddle, that Bud Sprague, the Army tackle, was up on the line of scrimmage, not three yards back as in the first half. Quick as a flash, Edwards called for Flanagan's favorite off-tackle play. Wallace blocked Tom Sprague in alone. Hearden, our right halfback, took Herbold, the Army end, out of the play. Then our right guard and quarterback deflected John Murrell, star Army fullback. Like a streak through this opening went Flanagan and reversed his field through the secondary, who were picked up by Ike Voedisch, John "Clipper" Smith and Fred Miller. It was a perfect day. Nobody laid a hand on Flanagan as he ran his 70 yards for a touchdown.

After this the two teams fought evenly until the finish. This one break settled the issue. Every coach plans his plays to score touchdowns, but they're generally spoiled by the defense. This was one practiced and well-planned play that worked.

The Army learned something from that. The very next game we played against Army, Chris Cagle, in an identical play, ran 45 yards against us for a touchdown. That likewise gave me a thrill — not of exhilaration but of exacerbation, for our tactics were perfectly reproduced by Mr. Cagle and Co.

Melodramatic intrusion of a planned and practiced play at a time and place not planned, or practiced, gave Parisien his greatest moment of gridiron glory. In the gorgeous setting of the Southern California stadium we, as guests, had, I thought, our hosts comfortably in the bag. The score was 7 to 6 in Notre Dame's favor and I sat on the bench murmuring *tempus fugit* and hoping it would fugit a little quicker. Suddenly the wind veered from behind us and came off the Graham McNamee mountains laden with the aroma of citrus groves. It stirred and stimulated the nostrils of the Los Angeles lads who awoke sharply to a realization of what was expected of them. Williams, their tailback, went right through our line for a touchdown. Our regular guards had been exhausted from the heat and a smart Southern California quarterback picked on the subs. The kick failed. The score was 12 to 7 in favor of Southern California.

As we lined up to receive the kickoff there were four minutes to play, with Southern California a raging torrent. We received the kickoff. It went for a touchback and was our ball on the 20-yard line. Heat had taken other tolls. Flanagan and a regular quarterback had left the game before this. Notre Dame tried three plays and failed. John Niemiec then punted 60 yards down the field. During those three plays I saw ten Notre Dame players still trying, giving the best of themselves, doggedly digging in. But the sub quarterback had an air of resignation. Hope as regards this game had left him. Remember, he was only a boy.

Southern California, who had taken Williams out, tried two plays, then kicked the ball back to us as though to say: "There it is, what are you going to do with it?"

I turned to Parisien, a little French quarterback who'd been injured during the year and hadn't played since. I said, "Art, how do you feel?"

He said, "Great."

"Well," I said, "do you think if you went in there you might try those two left-handed passes of yours, Numbers 83 and 84, and maybe pull this game out of the fire yet?"

Before I'd finished talking, he had a head-gear on and as he ran from the bench for the field he called back to me, "Coach, it's a cinch."

This was not egotism. Just self-confidence. Parisien took the ball on our 30-yard line, with just a little over a minute left to play. The crowd was apathetic and some were leaving. Apparently, it was all over.

On the first play Parisien pulled a tricky spinner and skipped through center for 8 yards. He called for time out. You could see the boy's youthful eagerness imbuing his ten teammates. But I, nor anyone else on the Notre Dame bench, had any hope. We were just playing the last card.

On the next play, out of a whirling mass of players, came Parisien sprinting with the ball. Turning quick as a flash, he flicked a left-handed pass 30 yards to Niemiec who was tackled and floored by Cravath, ever-alert California center. Next came a tearing wide end run by Niemiec, which, while it didn't gain, was a maneuver for position for the following play. Our acting captain called to the field judge, "How much time?"

"Thirty seconds," called the field judge.

Parisien's staccato bark rang out. The ball was passed, and again, out of a mass of players, Parisien sprinted. Again his left hand flicked a pass of 30 yards to the nimble Niemiec who crossed Southern California's goal line for the winning touchdown.

Eighty thousand people sat in that warm afternoon air, frozen with the thrill of that play. No sweeter balm has ever come to a coach's heart. It all goes to show what can be done by one Frenchman backed up by nine Irishmen and a German, none of whom know when they're beaten.

Similarly, a great Army backfield led by Light Horse Harry Wilson pulled a game out of the fire in the classic between Army and Navy when they met at Soldier Field, Chicago, in 1926.

The Army had been outcharged, outmaneuvered and outplayed by a relentless Navy team. As dusk gathered over the field the score stood 20 to 13 in favor of Navy. With defeat staring them in the face this great Army backfield moved up the field and at the crucial moment Nave, the Army quarterback, called for a cutback by Wilson — his favorite play. There was no hole there, but Wilson made one. He just handcuffed the two Navy linemen who tried to hang on to him. Into the open he sprang. He slapped his hip into the Navy fullback, sidestepped the Navy quarterback, reversed his field, up and over the goal line. Murrell kicked and the score was tied 20 to 20. It was a game of thrills — of the most unusual football, but to me, as I sat watching this kaleidoscopic, lightning-like drama which put first one then the other team ahead — this last, determined, do-or-die drive by Wilson stood out.

Accidents can crowd thrills into a game even more than design. Against Minnesota in 1926, Joe Boland, left tackle for

Notre Dame, in trying to block a punt had his leg broken by one of his own teammates. It was our ball. On the first play after that, Freddy Collins, our fullback, hit the line. Result — his jaw was broken in three places and out he came to take his place in the ambulance alongside Boland. After replacing both men I didn't know whether to swoon or laugh idiotically at these savage breaks. The teams lined up and on our next play Bucky Dahman, right halfback, ran 70 yards for a touchdown. I came down to earth. Over the telephone came a message from Boland and Collins, "We're all through," they said. "All we can do is get the score when the game's over."

I repeated the message to the team. Result: on the first play of the second half, Flanagan ran 70 yards for a touchdown.

For supper that night I ate nothing but celery — for my nerves.

The following year there were more thrills from Doc Spears' steamroller team. Niemiec scored early in the game. It looked as if Flanagan might cut loose at any moment, but the Gopher tackling was sure and tenacious. It completely nullified our running attack.

There were two minutes to play and we had the ball on our own 15-yard line. Having in mind killing time — 7 to 0 in our favor — the quarterback called for a line plunge. There was a fumble. Like a flash a big Minnesota tackle, Bronko Nagurski, pounced on the ball. It was Minnesota's ball on our 5-yard line! A minute and a half to play. Three times the great Joesting hit the Irish line, but he netted only a yard. It was fourth down, goal to go, and time was almost up — touchdown or the game was over. Back came the ball to Joesting. He started forward as if to plunge, but suddenly backed up and hurled a beautiful pass to Walsh, Minnesota right end, who jumped up into the air and caught it in the end zone. The score was 7 to 6.

Pharmer, the Minnesota sub halfback, kicked for the extra point, leisurely but surely, tying the score.

I don't know just what my feelings were. Spears' team was just as good as ours — tie score seemed fair. But at least I wasn't as phlegmatic as the Scotch manager of the Minnesota team. It was freezing cold, so he had purchased 10-cent gloves for the Minnesota subs to wear on the sidelines. When Minnesota tied the score, every Minnesota sub, plus scores of enthusiastic alumni, were leaping up and down in their glee, like Indians doing a war dance. All but the Scotch manager. He was busy picking up the 10-cent gloves which the subs had shed in their orgy of eurhythmic rapture.

A football coach rarely has a chance to watch a game where he is not nervous over the result, or vitally interested. But as I watched the Cornell-Penn game in 1924, my interest began from a purely technical viewpoint. It ended differently.

Before the game, in his room, Gil Dobie, the Cornell coach, had regaled me with eloquent pessimism. I used up two handkerchiefs crying with him over his doleful outlook regarding this game with his ancient rival. He was a poor optimist, but a good prophet. Penn won 20 to 0, which doesn't tell the quality of the game, as Cornell, aside from fumbles, played well. They might even have won the game for the sensational defensive playing of Kreuz, the Penn fullback. Here was a man who backed up a line in a manner to delight the heart of any coach. With a keen analytical eye he was never fooled. And how he loved to tackle! Once when it looked as though Cornell was going to score and Dobie's three-up-and-out play was functioning with machine-like regularity, Kreuz tackled so hard that the Cornell ball carrier fumbled.

Twice Kreuz did it. That was the test of his greatness. It was a tough break for Cornell. Kreuz made the break. The Penn quarterback and halfbacks were sensationally flashy. But Kreuz had the keen technique in which the intitiated spectator reveled.

There are the situations, too, in which the initiate or so-called expert — as a coach — does not revel. A good Notre Dame team was literally swept off its feet by a good Northwestern team in 1925. It shouldn't have been. I was disgusted. At the half the score was 10 to 0, favor of Northwestern. In the dressing room I said to those ineffective Notre Dame athletes, "I'm through. They call you the Fighting Irish. You're more like a bunch of peace-loving Swedes. But my name won't be connected with you any longer. We're on our home field, where Notre Dame hasn't been defeated in 20 years. You'll be able to tell your grandchildren you had that distinction — of laying down and getting licked for the first time in a generation on this field."

I turned to my assistant — Hunk Anderson.

"You take charge, Hunk," I said. "I'm through."

I walked away. As I got on the field a breeze hit me. It was the team passing out for the second half.

Down the field they went from the kickoff — 80 yards for a score. Down they went again — 80 yards again, and another score. Only three types of play were used in these marches for touchdown, Flanagan and Enright alternately carrying the ball. In the final period, with the score 13 to 10, I replaced these lads — they were utterly exhausted. They had staged the superb thrill of a triumphant comeback.

Not to overlook a play I did not see — for I couldn't be there — refer to Red Grange's four touchdowns in the first quarter of a game against Michigan in 1924. It stands out as a superb individual feat. Nothing quite like that has ever been seen in big-league football, although I encountered a one-man team phenomenon myself when Elmer Oliphant of Army ran Notre Dame ragged in 1916. Although we were hopelessly beaten, 30 to 10, I sat and marveled at the versatility and slashing brilliance of this magnificent Army back. If anybody asks me who was the greatest player the Army ever had, my vote goes to Oliphant.

Hardly less of a thrillmaker was Ernie Nevers of Stanford in the 1925 Tournament of Roses game. Nevers could do everything. He tore our line to shreds, ran the ends, forward-passed and kicked. True, we held him on one occasion for four downs on the 1-yard line; but by that time Nevers was exhausted and I had sent in two fresh guards and a fresh tackle — almost as good as the regulars — to stop this fury in football boots. Nevers labored mightily that day — and 80,000 people who saw the game do not realize that he was really entitled to a better break than 27 to 10. But for unwise quarterback play that great Stanford fullback would have turned in different figures.

Twice Stanford came 50 yards down the field with Nevers lugging the ball for first down after first down. Twice out of a clear sky the quarterback would call for a dangerous pass play thrown to one side so that it couldn't be covered, which, on each occasion, was intercepted by Layden and converted into a touchdown for Notre Dame. What would have happened had they allowed Nevers to continue lugging the ball right down over the goal line? But, when you hear of mistakes by quarterbacks or any backs or linemen, remember they're boys about 19 years of age, so what right has the spectator to ask for the mentality of a master mind of industry? I'm told they, too, sometimes make mistakes.

Just as a coach winces when he sees a faulty quarterback, so he thrills at a great quarterback — even when this lad's fighting him. Harpster of Carnegie Tech gave me heart-jumps in 1928. After the kickoff, he saw Freddy Collins, with a broken arm in a cast, limping badly, and in the first play he threw a forward pass to Rosensweig, who had run past Collins for the first touchdown. This was before I could remove Collins. Two minutes later, he saw our defensive guard way out of position and he sent Rosensweig on an end around play. Rosensweig cut back through that gap for another touchdown. I sent in a new guard and plugged up that gap, but the harm had all been done. Harpster had done the thinking first. A great passer, a great punter, a great returner of punts — he had also the supreme confidence of a fine quarterback, his only fault being that he sometimes took chances when it wasn't necessary.

Naturally, teams take advantage of disabled players, but rarely do they violate the football code by purposely punishing a man apparently hurt. On the contrary, there is always a display of gallantry on the field. In 1915 our center, Hugh O'Donnell, had a broken rib. He was to play against McEwen of Army, supposed to be one of the roughest centers in football. Harry Tuttle, the Army trainer, heard of this injury and came in with a special pad for O'Donnell. Just as play began, McEwen asked O'Donnell, "Which side is the broken rib on?"

O'Donnell pointed to it. There were 60 minutes of hard football, but not once did any Army player, least of all McEwen, touch O'Donnell's broken rib.

The code of football is — take advantage of a cripple by running around him on forward passing, but never hurt him.

Big schools give the big thrills — but they can come in small school games. Often in an obscure place a great player will shine, unknown to headlines. Such a man was Lamb, quarterback of Lombard, who played against Notre Dame in 1924. He was the mighty atom of football. He weighed 150 pounds and could do everything — an exceedingly dangerous man in open field. Against the Four Horsemen, after 25 minutes with Lamb running us ragged, we could score only one touchdown. His spunk and daring were captivating. Where we had expected a trial pushover, we had a real football game that challenged all our resources. Accidentally, on a head-on tackle, this versatile human whirlwind had his knee wrenched and had to leave the game. Immediately the game changed to a romp and Notre Dame added 40 points.

But while the gridiron game is essentially amateur, pro football has its thrills — and I'm one champion of amateur sport who will never deny it. I'd never seen Benny Friedman play with Michigan so I took advantage of a chance to see this famed quarterback play pro football against the Chicago Bears. It was an afternoon of thrills at the miraculous dexterity of his passing. Four yards, 10 yards, 40 yards — harassed and pounded — he threw the ball from all angles, standing or running at terrific speed, hitting his target right on the button — with never a miss. There are those who say Friedman is the greatest passer of all time. They're not far wrong. He could hit a dime at 40 yards. Besides being a great passer he hit the line, tackled, blocked and did everything that a fine football player should do.

In grading thrills of gridiron action an experienced observer has difficulties. But I sat in the stands at Atlanta one afternoon and saw a magnificent Notre Dame team that seemed headed for its annual victory over Georgia Tech suddenly recoil before the furious pounding of one man — Pund, center. Nobody could stop him. Notre Dame fought like tigers — but this man was a tiger tamer. I counted 20 scoring plays that this man ruined. Our boys fought in the sun and heat. With this giant dervish shattering them it was a sight for the gods. We were hopelessly beaten — but I had the thrill of my life to see great fighters go down in defeat before a greater fighter.

Endlessly, the sights and sounds of the most exciting of all games, with the blare of bands, the waving pennants, the cheering crowds, convey the lesson that my young friend who called on me in the name of culture should remember. Football is clean sport, which is as much a part of culture as clean literature.

Wellington said that the battle of Waterloo was won on the playing fields of Eton. I'm no Wellington, but I firmly believe that America's future battles, in peace and in war, are being won on the gridirons of the country.

THE DAY KNUTE ROCKNE DIED
by William L. White

On a wind-swept promontory of the Flint Hills, out of sight
of any vestige of human habitation, lies the twisted wreckage of
a giant Fokker, its three motors buried deep in the stony soil,
which carried to death Knute Rockne, the Viking of football,
two pilots and five other passengers.

The Flint Hills, marking the boundary between the cornfields
of Eastern Kansas and the ocean of wheat to the west, are a
lonely and desolate out-cropping of hard limestone ridges which
run two hundred miles from north to south across the state. A
few isolated villages and ranch houses dot its gentle valleys and
every spring hundreds of thousands of cattle come up from the
Texas ranges to be fattened for market on the virgin prairie sod,
untouched by plow, which in a few weeks will be green with the
spring rains.

A few miles away, almost within sight of the twisted fuselage
of the trimotored Fokker, run the abandoned ruts of the old
stage road cut by stage coaches in the eighteen-fifties and sixties,
which ran between the ancient federal military posts of Fort
Leavenworth and Fort Sill, five hundred miles apart.

Among the first to reach the wreckage was R. Z. Blackburn,
who was feeding his cattle in a pasture. He heard the roar of the

morning mail plane. It is just at this point in the Flint Hills that the old stage road, marked by furrows in the prairie sod, intersects with the transcontinental air mail line marked by flashing beacon lights, running between Kansas City and Wichita.

The hum of airplane motors was a familiar sound to Blackburn. Today the plane was invisible above the gray clouds which hung a scant one thousand feet above the Flint Hills. After dying away in the fog, the hum returned and attracted his attention. Something apparently was wrong with the regular morning mail plane. He looked up from his work in time to see the silver Fokker drop like a plummet from the low-hanging clouds. Behind it fluttered a severed silver wing.

Its motors still roaring, the Fokker disappeared behind a hill, there was a splintering thud and the motors ceased. Blackburn saw the severed wing twisting lightly down through the air. It came to ground half a mile to the east of the plane.

Leaving his work, Blackburn hurried over the hill, but first to reach the scene was Edward Baker, a ranchman's son, who was finishing his chores when he saw the roaring Fokker spin down from the low clouds.

One look at the twisted wreckage lying strangely silent on the brow of the hill, and Edward turned his wiry little cow pony back toward the ranch, where the news of the disaster reached Cottonwood Falls via a humming rural telephone line.

News via the rural telephone party wires travels fast, even in the Flint Hills. Almost before the two ambulances arrived from Cottonwood Falls, the ranchmen were galloping over the hills toward the stony promontory on which the plane lay in the stillness on the prairie. But an hour later the world closed in. First, two ambulances arrived and picked up the mangled bodies.

Then streams of motor cars from the nearby villages of Bazaar, Matfield Green, Cottonwood Falls and Strong City were on roads. Ranchers' wives and children trudging from the road in the valley to the scene of the wreck were guided by the tail of the plane, jutting high from the hill on the horizon.

The sheriff, the county attorney, the coroner and village correspondents for the big town newspapers rushed to the scene.

A team of mules from a ranch pulled the remainder of the fuselage from the hole plowed in the ground. Three more bodies were separated from the wreckage.

An hour passed, then early in the afternoon as the news spread to the cities that a mail plane was down and Knute Rockne was dead, airplanes from Wichita zoomed overhead, swooped like great birds curiously inspecting a wounded fellow and settled unsteadily on neighboring hills. They taxied excitedly toward the tangled torn fabric and twisted metal on the hill top. Five or six had arrived by mid-afternoon. Khaki-clad pilots jumped from cockpits, removed leather helmets, ruefully inspected the wreckage and walked half a mile east to look at the mangled wing.

First driving away a crowd of excited overgrown boys who were tearing off bits of fabric for souvenirs, the pilots gathered in knots to discuss in low voices the probable cause of the disaster while the crowd of country men clustered about them in a vain attempt to catch a few words.

It was a weird scene. The twisted wreckage on the hilltop; the half-dozen visiting airplanes from Wichita and Kansas City drawn up nearby; cowboys viewing the tangled aluminum from their saddles, their ponies stamping nervously at the unfamiliar odor of gasoline, fabric paint and splintered wood; an endless stream of curiosity seekers trudging from their motor cars parked along the road.

The idling crowd remained for perhaps an hour to gape, gathering in knots about the eyewitness and almost eyewitnesses to the crash to hear the varying accounts of the disaster, tugging at the wreckage to bend off a bit of fabric or a sliver of wood as a souvenir. Then the men and women trudged back across the marshy prairie grass to the roads. The mangled bodies of the victims lay in the two undertaking establishments at Cottonwood Falls.

In the clothing of the body of the great Notre Dame coach were found papers and letters identifying him. Even before the passenger list of the Fokker arrived from the company's headquarters in Kansas City, a passenger list was found in the pocket of the pilot, whose body had been cut loose from the straps which bound it to the seat.

Meanwhile three girls sat at the switchboard of the telephone office of Cottonwood Falls talking to Universal City, Chicago and New York, and listened to grief-stricken voices of fathers and wives, in Chicago, California and Connecticut as they asked falteringly for the details which they dreaded to hear, and pleaded for some hint of hope when there was none to give.

As for the cause of the accident, the few known facts are clear; the plane fell because of the broken wing, which was already severed when it appeared from the clouds. There was no hint of fire, not so much as a scorch on the wrecked fabric, and, strangely enough, the shock of the crash did not ignite the gasoline which drenched the prairie sod around the wreck.

Whatever happened is known only to the pilot and to the gray overhanging clouds, which drifted off to the Southwest, carrying the secret of the death of Knute Rockne and his seven companions in its chill gossamer bosom.

So died the great Viking of football on a high hill overlooking a prairie, at the crossroads of the old forgotten stage road and the new highway of the air, and at his bier keeping vigil on the hill top stood, not the Four Horsemen of Notre Dame, but four sun-tanned horsemen of the plains forcing back from the tangled wreckage a gaping curious crowd.

Swiftly and painlessly he passed from a land of far horizons into a horizon without bounds.

A PRESIDENTIAL SALUTE
by Ronald Reagan
President of the United States
March 9, 1988

Thank you... Moose, when I was young and reading about George Gipp, I never thought I'd come back as the Gipper. Well, thank you, Reverend Malloy, and Governor, Lieutenant Governor, distinguished guests, and a special hello to the Rockne family.

I brought with me Dick Lyng, our Secretary of Agriculture and Notre Dame's representative in the Cabinet. And the five — not the four horsemen — from Congress — South Bend's own Jack Hiler, our quarterback in this effort, and four other distinguished alumni — Joe McDade, Dan Lungren, Dave Martin and Ben Blaz.

It's a pleasure to visit once again the home of the Fighting Irish. With St. Patrick's Day coming up, and after seeing those film clips, it brings to mind another deathbed scene. You know, apparently the town rogue of one small Irish hamlet lay on his deathbed as the priest prepared for the atonement. "Do you renounce the devil? Do you renounce him and all his works?" the priest asked. And the rogue opened one eye and said, "Father, this is no time for making enemies."

It's great to be back here. I've said this before, but I want you to know the first time I ever saw Notre Dame was when I came here as a sports announcer, two years out of college, to broadcast a football game. You won or I wouldn't have mentioned it.

And then, of course, I was here with Pat O'Brien and a whole host of Hollywood stars for the world premiere of *Knute Rockne: All-American.* Now let me explain, I may be saying the name differently, but when we made the picture we were told, and Bonnie upheld it to us, that it was *Ka-nute* — not *nute.* So you'll have to get used to me saying it that way. *Knute Rockne: All-American.* How I had wanted to make that movie and play the part of George Gipp.

Of course, the role was a young actor's dream; it had a great entrance, an action middle, and a death scene right out of the opera. But it was more than that. I know that, to many of you today, Rockne is a revered name, a symbol of greatness and, yes, a face now on a postage stamp. But my generation, well, we actually knew the legend as it happened — we saw it unfold. And we felt it was saying something important about us as a people and a nation. And there was little room for skepticism or cynicism; we knew the legend was based on fact.

I would like to interject here if I could that it's difficult to stand before you and make you understand how great that legend was at that time. It isn't just a memory here and of those who knew him, but throughout this nation he was a living legend. Millions of Americans just automatically rooted for him on Saturday afternoon and rooted, therefore, for Notre Dame.

Now, of course, the Rockne legend stood for fair play and honor but, you know, it was thoroughly American in another way. It was practical; it placed a value on devastating quickness and agility and on confounding the opposition with good old American cleverness. But, most of all, the Rockne legend meant this — when you think about it, it's what's been taught here at Notre Dame since her founding — that on or off the field, it is faith that makes the difference, it is faith that makes great things happen.

And believe me, it took faith, and a lot of it, for an unknown actor to think that he could get the part of George Gipp. I was under contract to Warner Brothers, but I had been all over the studio talking about my idea for a story. Having come from sports announcing to the movies, I said I thought that the movies ought to make the life story of Knute Rockne. And then one day I picked up the *Daily Variety* and read where Warner Brothers was announcing that they were making the life story of Knute Rockne and were starting to cast the film. Well, all I'd ever wanted was to play the Gipper if they some day made the film. And I approached Pat O'Brien, who was going to play Rockne — he'd been my choice — and he told me bluntly that I talked too much and that's where Warner Brothers got the idea. And I told him what my ambition was and he said, "Well, they're looking for a name actor." But Pat did intervene with the head of the studio, the top producer, Hal Wallis. Hal was, to put it mildly, unimpressed with my credentials.

He started by telling me I didn't look big enough for the part. Well, I wasn't very polite because I told him, "You're producing the picture and you don't know that George Gipp weighed five pounds less than I weigh right now. He walked with a kind of slouch and almost a limp. He looked like a football player only when he was on the field." And then I went home because they told me some cameramen had told me that the fellas in the front office, they only knew what they saw on film. And I dug down in the trunk and came up with my own pictures of myself playing football in college and brought them back and showed them to Hal Wallis. Well, he finally let me do a test for the part and Pat O'Brien, knowing of my nervousness and desire, graciously agreed to be a part of it and play in the scene with me. Well, of course, I had an advantage, I had known George Gipp's story for years and the lines were straight from Knute Rockne's diary. And the test scene was one that said something about what

Rockne liked to see in his players. It was George Gipp's first practice. You saw that scene where he was told to get into uniform. And Rockne told him to carry the ball, and Gipp just looked back at Rockne, and cocked an eyebrow and said, "How far?"

Well, I mentioned all this because, as I say, Knute liked spirit in his ballplayers. Grantland Rice tells us that once when he was working with the four backfield stars who became known as "The Four Horsemen," the fellow named Jimmy Crowley just couldn't get it right. Now, you know, I never tell ethnic jokes anymore unless they're about the Irish. But in view of the spirit of this occasion, maybe I can be permitted some leeway. Rockne, who, by the way, was Norwegian, was commonly called "the Swede." He finally got exacerbated after Crowley muffed a play, and hollered, "What's dumber than a dumb Irishman?" And without missing a beat, Crowley shot right back, "A smart Swede."

Well, that was Rockne. And you know, not too long ago I was questioned about the George Gipp story. And this interviewer had really done his research. In fact, he'd even gone back and talked to my old football coach, Ralph McKenzie, at Eureka College who was 91 years old, and asked him about my football career. Well, now I've been through a lot of interviews but, believe me, I tensed up at hearing that. And apparently Mac described me as "eager, aggressive, better on defense, overall an average football player — but an outstanding talker."

Well, anyway, I was asked whether I knew that George Gipp was no angel, that he played in some pool games and card games in his time. And, of course, that was true and I said so. But it was also true of George Gipp — and it is legitimately part of the legend — that he used his winnings from those games to buy food for destitute families and to help other students pay their way through Notre Dame. And the reason he got so sick and later died from pneumonia was because he had promised a former teammate who had become a high school coach that he would give his students some pointers. Author James Cox tells us it was during that training session in Chicago that an icy wind blew in across Lake Michigan and the Gipper first felt the ache and sore throat that would lead to the illness that would take his life. You see, there were no miracle drugs in those days. And a promising young life was ended; but the point is, George Gipp couldn't forget a friend.

And I've always thought that it was no mere coincidence that the legend of George Gipp and Knute Rockne emerged from this great institution of higher learning. Not simply because of its academic excellence, but because it stands among the winds of subjectivity for lasting values and principles that are the heart of our civilization, and on which all human progress is built. Notre Dame not only educates its students in the development of honesty, courage, and all the other things we call character. Rockne once wrote, "Sportsmanship means fair play. It means having a little respect for the other fellow's point of view. It means a real application of the Golden Rule." And I know a fine example of this is the charitable care 80 of you students give the handicapped children at the Logan Center. This and other acts of good will say much about your generation.

There are those who suggest the 1980s have been characterized by greed. Well, charitable giving is up. I think our detractors are looking in the wrong places. If they want to see the goodness and love of life of this generation, the commitment to decency and a better future, let them come here...to Notre Dame. It's a place where the Golden Rule, the legend of Rockne, and the idea of religious faith still live.

Rockne stressed character. He knew, instinctively, the relationship between the physical and moral. That is as true of nations as it is of people. Charles Lindbergh, also a hero of that time, once said, "Short-term survival may depend on the knowledge of nuclear physicists and the performance of supersonic aircraft, but long-term survival depends alone on the character of man.''

Rockne believed in competition. Yet, he did not rely on brute force for winning the victory. Instead, he's remembered as the man who brought ingenuity, speed and agility into this most American of sports.

May I interrupt myself here for a second and tell you something else about him? As a sports announcer, I was told by many of the great coaches in this land whose teams had played against Notre Dame teams under Rockne, that one of their hardest problems when playing Notre Dame was that their team worshipped Rockne — that they were fans of his, and that when they came out in the field, the first thing they looked for was, where was this great, great coach.

Rockne, you see, was a man of vision. And that's how he came by his reputation as someone ''larger than life'' and a ''miracle man.'' Because of his tremendous success in sports, it's easy to forget that he was something else as well, something not too many people knew about him. He was also a man of science, having taught chemistry here at Notre Dame for four years. I must believe that he would not be at all surprised at the enormous advances that have taken place over the five decades since his death.

Much has been said about the technological revolution in which we are living. Every time we turn around, it seems to be staring us in the face. Typewriters are being replaced in corporate offices throughout the country by highly efficient word processors. With the almost universal proliferation of copy machines, carbon paper has almost gone the way of the buggy whip. Not only deregulation, but design and technology have made our airlines more efficient.

The American workplace, in recent years, has undergone a dramatic transformation. Just in the last 5 years, manufacturing productivity of our working people has increased 4.7 percent annually. And from the plant floor to the corporate boardroom, there is more cooperation, a sense of common purpose, more of a winning spirit, and state of the art equipment and machinery available to do the job. I've seen it in the many companies that I've visited all across this nation, and I've heard it from the working people themselves. And don't let all the gloom and doomers tell you any different. There's a will to succeed evident in our land. I happen to have always believed in the American people. Don't ever sell them short. Given the proper tools and a level playing ground, our workers can out-produce and out-compete anyone, anywhere.

It's a far different picture than the agonizing sight of a decade ago, when many were counting out American workers and American industry. We were told that Americans would no longer go the extra mile, no longer had the drive to excel; that our country was in decline and that we, as a people, should lower our expectations.

Well, today, we see an America ready to compete, anxious to compete. In fact, our workers are so productive that foreign companies are opening plants in the United States, sometimes to manufacture products for export to other countries. Our industrial base, contrary to a totally false yet widespread impression, is strong and, in fact, is growing. We've added almost 300,000 manufacturing jobs in the last six months, and that trend is continuing. There are over 19 million manufacturing jobs today, about the same as the last 20 years, while manufacturing output is up almost 40 percent over the last 5 years. And unemployment continues to decline. In short, American industry is lean and mean and ready to meet the competition head on. I predict that, as this year progresses, we will see American manufacturing re-emerge as the leading force in the world marketplace. Exports will, in fact, race ahead and lead our domestic economy.

What is propelling our country forward? That fundamental

element of the American character that no tyranny and a few of our competitors can ever hope to match. Knute Rockne knew and appreciated it — the creative genius and omnipresent optimism of our people. We had faith in them these last seven years, and they did the rest. That's why, instead of giving up, we set our sights high. We didn't raise taxes, drain the investment pool, and tell our working people and business leaders to hunker down and prepare for the worst, to lower their expectations. We asked them to dream great dreams, to reach for the stars.

We left resources in the private sector that others would have drained into the bureaucracy. The heavy investment made in our economy during the early part of this decade is paying off now, in a big way. President Franklin Roosevelt once said, "The only limit on our realization of tomorrow will be our doubts of today." Well, together, we, the American people, have proven the doubters wrong, time and again. We've done it by keeping our eyes on the future, by setting our sights on what can be done rather than on complaining about how much there is to do. We've done it by viewing every problem as an opportunity. I happen to believe in something former astronaut John Swigert once said, "Technology and commitment can overcome any challenge."

The individual investment made in companies, large and small; the retraining of our work force to handle the jobs in this technological age; the search for new ideas and innovative approaches; the modernization of older industries and investment in the new; energy, creativity, and yes, hard work on a massive scale throughout our country, from the bottom up — this is the foundation of our prosperity and the impetus for national progress.

Our program has been to foster innovation and to keep our country in the forefront of change. And that's why last year we committed ourselves to building the world's largest particle accelerator, superconducting super-collider to maintain our leadership in high-energy physics research and America's scientific and technological competitiveness. That's why we're developing a space plane that by the end of the century will take off from a runway, but once at high altitude will rocket into near space and zip to its destination at 10, and even 20 times the speed of sound.

And that's why I'm proposing to Congress in my Fiscal Year '89 budget a new Thomas A. Edison prize program offering monetary awards to any American who can develop workable, groundbreaking technologies that could improve our quality of life. And that's why scientists right here at Notre Dame are blazing trails in superconductivity research, finding ways so that this breakthrough technology can be put to use for the betterment of all mankind. Because someday, because of research being done here, transcontinental railroads will slide heavy cargoes on a magnetic cushion, cheaply and quickly across the country; perhaps our energy costs will drop below anything we could have imagined a decade ago. Rockne exemplified the American spirit of never giving up. That spirit is the reason why you and your generation are going to succeed. That is why we're not just going to compete, we're going to win.

And that's also why this year we'll see the return of the American Space Shuttle, symbolic of America's tenacity. We never give up. And I cannot help but believe that the heroes of the Challenger will be cheering along with the rest of us when the United States reclaims its rightful leadership role in leading the conquest of this, the last frontier.

Technology in these last decades has reshaped our lives. It's opened vast opportunity for the common man and has brought all of mankind into one community. Today, worldwide communications and transportation have linked productive citizens of every free land. Through advances in medicine, our people are living longer, and the quality of their later years has been vastly improved. I like to remind people that I've already lived some 23 years longer than the average life expectancy when I was born. That's a source of frustration to a number of people.

And you know there are always those who say the problem's too big, it can't be helped, let's prepare for the worst. But a few years ago, we heard that about the drug problem here in America. But a few people, including my roommate Nancy, said it was time for action, not gloom and doom. And the statistics are starting to show what her commitment and the commitment of millions of others have accomplished. Not only did a recent survey of high school seniors show that one-third fewer seniors acknowledged current use of cocaine in 1987 than the year before, but almost all the students said it was wrong to even try a drug like cocaine. We still have a long way to go, and when Nancy and I see stories saying just that in the newspaper, we welcome them. But let's also remember that the shock of recognition is not a sign of defeat, it's the beginning of victory. And victory will be ours; and I hope that each of you will join us in saying that drugs hurt, drugs kill, that each of us must "Just Say No" to drugs and drug users. And most of all, in giving America what America deserves — your very best — and that means a drug-free generation. And may I challenge you? Why not? Why not make your generation the one that said, once and for all, no more drugs in the United States of America, or the world.

Excellence too is returning to our schools. We've learned what's always been known here at Notre Dame — that values are an essential part of educational excellence. Throughout the nation, parents and teachers are gaining greater control over local curriculums, emphasizing basics and making their children's education a priority in all of our lives. And they're right to do so because all of the wonderful gains I've talked about so far — especially those gains built on the growth of technology — depend on young Americans who know how to think, calculate, write and communicate.

Now, there are those who see a dark side to our technological progress. Yes, they admit our well-being has been enhanced in so many ways. Technological advances, now, are making it more likely, for example, that our natural resources will be spared as long-haul telephone lines and electrical cable give way to the satellite transmissions and computer chips. I spoke to the young people of Europe not long ago via our Worldnet system and reminded them that only a short time ago such a transmission would have required thousands of tons of copper wire and other resources. Instead, our talk was transmitted quickly, cheaply, efficiently, almost miraculously from our continent to theirs, via satellite. Yet it is pointed out that, regretfully, as man has advanced into this new age, so has his capability to kill and destroy; and it's no longer just those in uniform who are victimized.

In World War I, more than eight million military personnel lost their lives and over 12 million civilians died. During the Second World War, almost 20 million in uniform lost their lives; however, there were about 14 million civilians killed. And if there's ever another such conflagration, a Third World War, hundreds of millions will lose their lives, and it's estimated that 90 percent of the casualties will be civilian.

When I was in college, I remember a debate in one of my classes. This was back in the days when the bomber was just being recognized as the potent weapon that it later became in the post-World War I days. Our class debated whether or not Americans — people who, to our way of thinking, stood for high moral standards — would ever drop bombs from an airplane on a city. And the class was about evenly divided, half felt it might be necessary, the others felt bombing civilians would always be beyond the pale of decency, totally unacceptable human conduct, no matter how heinous the enemy. Well, a decade later, few, if any, who had been in that room objected to our country's wholesale bombing of cities. Civilization's standards of morality had changed. The thoughts of killing more and more people, noncombatants, became more and more acceptable.

Well, today, technology is pointing toward a way out of this dilemma. It's given us the promise of basing our security in the future on protection rather than the threat of retaliation. SDI offers a chance to reverse not only the nuclear arms build-up, but also to reverse the trend that in effect has put a lower and lower value on human life. Technology offers you young people, who debate in today's classroom, an option that threatens no one and offers a shield rather than ever sharper, more deadly swords. It offers you young people a chance to raise the moral standards of mankind. When I came here in 1981 for one of the first major addresses of my presidency, I acknowledged the difficulties we faced in the world, not only the threat of nuclear war but also totalitarian expansion around the world especially in places like Afghanistan. But I also said that in avoiding these two unacceptable choices of nuclear confrontation or totalitarian rule, the West had a secret resource of strength — the spiritual values of our civilization and the essential decency and optimism of our peoples.

And something that got a warm response from you undergraduates, but was treated very skeptically in Washington, was my suggestion that these values were so strong and this inner strength was so great that, in the long run, the West would not contain communism — we would transcend communism; that the era of the nuclear threat and totalitarian darkness would someday be put behind us; that we would look again with all the people of the Earth to the bright, sunlit uplands of world peace, world prosperity, and yes, world freedom. How much has changed since those days, and, as we look back at seven years of peace as well as progress in arms reductions and the hope of a Soviet exit from Afghanistan, we can be pleased that the inner strength of our nation and our civilization is increasingly apparent with every day that passes.

And that inner strength — that inner strength is what Notre Dame and the legend of Rockne are all about. You know, so much is said about Rockne's influence on his ballplayers but actually he liked to talk about their influence on him. In his autobiography, he described his inability to sleep one night before a big game. So he was up early in the lobby and saw two of his boys come down the stairs and go out. And then others came and followed them. And though he had a pretty good idea of what was going on, he decided to follow along. "They didn't realize it," he said in his diary, "but these youngsters were making a powerful impression on me." And he said, "When I saw them walking up to the Communion rail to receive, and realized the hours of sleep they had sacrificed, I understood what a powerful ally their religion was to them in their work on the football field."

And after Rockne found — here at Notre Dame — his own religious faith, a friend of his at the University of Maryland asked him if he minded telling him about it. "Why should I mind telling you?" he said, "You know all this hurry and battling we're going through is just an expression of our inner selves striving for something else. The way I look at it is that we're all here to try and find, each in his own way, the best road to our ultimate goal. I believe I've found my way and I shall travel it to the end."

And travel it to the end he did. And when they found him in the Kansas cornfield where the plane had gone down, they also found next to him a prayer book and at his fingertips the Rosary of Notre Dame, the Rosary of Our Lady.

Someone put it so well at the time: Knute Rockne did more spiritual good than a thousand preachers. His career was a sermon in right living.

Yes, we've seen more change in the last 50 years — since

Knute Rockne was with us — than in all the other epics of history combined. You are the beneficiaries of this, and it is you who will continue the struggle and carry mankind to greater and greater heights. As Americans, as free people, you must stand firm, even when it's uncomfortable for you to do so. It won't always be easy. There will be moments of joy, of triumph. There will also be times of despair. Times when all those around you are ready to give up. It's then I want you to remember our meeting today and "Some time when the team is up against it and the breaks are beating the boys, tell them to go out there with all they've got and win just one for the Gipper. I don't know where I'll be then, but I'll know about it, and I'll be happy."

Good luck in the years ahead, and God bless you all. Thank you.

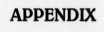

APPENDIX

APPENDIX A

ROCKNE'S NATIONAL CHAMPIONSHIPS AS A HEAD COACH

Season	Team Record
1919	9-0-0
1920	9-0-0
1924	10-0-0
1927	7-1-1
1929	9-0-0
1930	10-0-0

APPENDIX B

NOTRE DAME'S FOOTBALL
RECORD, 1910–1930

WITH ROCKNE AS PLAYER

1910

(4-1-1)
Coach: Frank C. Longman
Captain: Ralph Dimmick

Oct. 8	W	Olivet	48–0	H
Oct. 22	W	Butchel (Akron)	51–0	H
Nov. 5	L	Michigan State	0–17	A
Nov. 12	W	Rose Poly	41–3	A
Nov. 19	W	Ohio Northern	47–0	H
Nov. 24	T	Marquette	5–5	A
			192–25	

1911

(6-0-2)
Coach: John L. Marks
Captain: Luke L. Kelly

Oct. 7	W	Ohio Northern	32–6	H
Oct. 14	W	St. Viator	43–0	H
Oct. 21	W	Butler	27–0	H
Oct. 28	W	Loyola (Chi.)	80–0	H
Nov. 4	T	Pittsburgh	0–0	H
Nov. 11	W	St. Bonaventure	34–0	H
Nov. 20	W	Wabash	6–3	A
Nov. 30	T	Marquette	0–0	A
			222–9	

1912

(7-0-0)
Coach: John L. Marks
Captain: Charles E. (Gus) Dorais

Oct. 5	W	St. Viator	116–7	H
Oct. 12	W	Adrian	74–7	H
Oct. 19	W	Morris Harvey	39–0	H
Oct. 26	W	Wabash	41–6	H
Nov. 2	W	Pittsburgh	3–0	A
Nov. 9	W	St. Louis	47–7	A
Nov. 28	W	Marquette	69–0	N
			389–27	

1913

(7-0-0)
Coach: Jesse C. Harper
Captain: Knute K. Rockne

Oct. 4	W	Ohio Northern	87–0	H
Oct. 18	W	South Dakota	20–7	H
Oct. 25	W	Alma	62–0	H
Nov. 1	W	Army	35–13	A
Nov. 7	W	Penn State	14–7	A
Nov. 22	W	Christian Bros. (St.L.)	20–7	A
Nov. 27	W	Texas	30–7	A
			268–41	

WITH ROCKNE AS ASSISTANT COACH

1914

(6-2-0)
Coach: Jesse C. Harper
Captain: Keith K. Jones

Oct. 3	W	Alma	56-0	H
Oct. 10	W	Rose Poly	103-0	H
Oct. 17	L	Yale	0-28	A
Oct. 24	W	South Dakota	33-0	N1
Oct. 31	W	Haskell	20-7	H
Nov. 7	L	Army	7-20	A
Nov. 14	W	Carlisle	48-6	N2
Nov. 26	W	Syracuse	20-0	A
			287-61	

N1 — at Sioux Falls; N2 — at Chicago

1915

(7-1-0)
Coach: Jesse C. Harper
Captain: Freeman C. Fitzgerald

Oct. 2	W	Alma	32-0	H
Oct. 9	W	Haskell	34-0	H
Oct. 23	L	Nebraska	19-20	A
Oct. 30	W	South Dakota	6-0	H
Nov. 6	W	Army	7-0	A
Nov. 13	W	Creighton	41-0	A
Nov. 25	W	Texas	36-7	A
Nov. 27	W	Rice	55-2	A
			230-29	

1916

(8-1-0)
Coach: Jesse C. Harper
Captain: Stan Cofall

Sep. 30	W	Case Tech	48-0	H
Oct. 7	W	Western Reserve	48-0	A
Oct. 14	W	Haskell	26-0	H
Oct. 28	W	Wabash	60-0	H
Nov. 4	L	Army	10-30	A
Nov. 11	W	South Dakota	21-0	N
Nov. 18	W	Michigan State	14-0	A
Nov. 25	W	Alma	46-0	H
Nov. 30	W	Nebraska	20-0	A
			293-30	

N — at Sioux Falls

1917

(6-1-1)
Coach: Jesse C. Harper
Captain: James Phelan

Oct. 6	W	Kalamazoo	55-0	H
Oct. 13	T	Wisconsin	0-0	A
Oct. 20	L	Nebraska	0-7	A
Oct. 27	W	South Dakota	40-0	H
Nov. 3	W	Army	7-2	A
Nov. 10	W	Morningside	13-0	A
Nov. 17	W	Michigan State	23-0	H
Nov. 24	W	Wash. & Jefferson	3-0	A
			141-9	

WITH ROCKNE AS HEAD COACH

1918

(3-1-2)
Captain: Leonard Bahan

Sep. 28	W	Case Tech	26-6	A
Nov. 2	W	Wabash	67-7	A
Nov. 9	T	Great Lakes	7-7	H
Nov. 16	L	Mich. State	7-13	A
Nov. 23	W	Purdue	26-6	A
Nov. 28	T	Nebraska	0-0	A
			133-39	

1919

(9-0-0)
Captain: Leonard Bahan

Oct. 4	W	Kalamazoo	14-0	H	5,000
Oct. 11	W	Mount Union	60-7	H	4,000
Oct. 18	W	Nebraska	14-9	A	10,000
Oct. 25	W	Western St. Nor.	53-0	H	2,500
Nov. 1	W	Indiana	16-3	N	5,000
Nov. 8	W	Army	12-9	A	8,000
Nov. 15	W	Michigan State	13-0	H	5,000
Nov. 22	W	Purdue	33-13	A	7,000
Nov. 27	W	Morningside	14-6	A	10,000
			229-47		56,500

N — at Indianapolis

1920

(9-0-0)
Captain: Frank Coughlin

Oct. 2	W	Kalamazoo	39-0	H	5,000
Oct. 9	W	Western St. Nor.	42-0	H	3,500
Oct. 16	W	Nebraska	16-7	A	9,000
Oct. 23	W	Valparaiso	28-3	H	8,000
Oct. 30	W	Army	27-17	A	10,000
Nov. 6	W	Purdue	28-0	H	12,000
Nov. 13	W	Indiana	13-10	N	14,000
Nov. 20	W	*Northwestern	33-7	A	20,000
Nov. 25	W	Michigan State	25-0	A	8,000
			251-44		89,500

N — at Indianapolis
*George Gipp's last game. He contracted a strep throat and died from complications of the disease on December 14 at the age of 25.

1921

(10-1-0)
Captain: Edward N. Anderson

Sep. 24	W	Kalamazoo	56-0	H	8,000
Oct. 1	W	DePauw	57-10	H	8,000
Oct. 8	L	Iowa	7-10	A	7,500
Oct. 15	W	Purdue	33-0	A	7,500
Oct. 22	W	Nebraska	7-0	H	14,000
Oct. 29	W	Indiana	28-7	N1	10,000
Nov. 5	W	Army	28-0	A	7,000
Nov. 8	W	Rutgers	48-0	N2	12,000
Nov. 12	W	Haskell	42-7	H	5,000
Nov. 19	W	Marquette	21-7	A	11,000
Nov. 24	W	Michigan State	48-0	H	15,000
			375-41		105,000

N1 — at Indianapolis; N2 — at Polo Grounds

1922

(8-1-1)
Captain: Glen Carberry

Sep. 30	W	Kalamazoo	46-0	H	5,000
Oct. 7	W	St. Louis	26-0	H	7,000
Oct. 14	W	Purdue	20-0	A	9,000
Oct. 21	W	DePaul	34-7	H	5,000
Oct. 28	W	Georgia Tech	13-3	A	20,000
Nov. 4	W	Indiana	27-0	H	22,000
Nov. 11	T	Army	0-0	A	15,000
Nov. 18	W	Butler	31-3	A	12,000
Nov. 25	W	Carnegie Tech	19-0	A	30,000
Nov. 30	L	Nebraska	6-14	A	16,000
			222-27		141,000

1923

(9-1-0)
Captain: Harvey Brown

Sep. 29	W	Kalamazoo	74-0	H	10,000
Oct. 6	W	Lombard	14-0	H	8,000
Oct. 13	W	Army	13-0	N	30,000
Oct. 20	W	Princeton	25-2	A	30,000
Oct. 27	W	Georgia Tech	35-7	H	20,000
Nov. 3	W	Purdue	34-7	H	20,000
Nov. 10	L	Nebraska	7-14	A	30,000
Nov. 17	W	Butler	34-7	H	10,000
Nov. 24	W	Carnegie Tech	26-0	A	30,000
Nov. 29	W	St. Louis	13-0	A	9,000
			275-37		197,000

N — at Ebbets Field, Brooklyn

1924

(10–0–0)
Captain: Adam Walsh

Oct. 4	W	Lombard	40–0	H	8,000
Oct. 11	W	Wabash	34–0	H	10,000
Oct. 18	W	Army	13–7	N1	55,000
Oct. 25	W	Princeton	12–0	A	40,000
Nov. 1	W	Georgia Tech	34–3	H	22,000
Nov. 8	W	Wisconsin	38–3	A	28,425
Nov. 15	W	Nebraska	34–6	H	22,000
Nov. 22	W	Northwestern	13–6	N2	45,000
Nov. 29	W	Carnegie Tech	40–19	A	35,000
			258–44		265,425

ROSE BOWL

Jan. 1	W	Stanford	27–10	N3	c53,000

N1 — at Polo Grounds; N2 — at Soldier Field: N3 — at Pasadena, Calif.

1925

(7–2–1)
Captain: Clem Crowe

Sep. 26	W	Baylor	41–0	H	13,000
Oct. 3	W	Lombard	69–0	H	10,000
Oct. 10	W	Beloit	19–3	H	10,000
Oct. 17	L	Army	0–27	YS	65,000
Oct. 24	W	Minnesota	19–7	A	49,000
Oct. 31	W	Georgia Tech	13–0	A	12,000
Nov. 7	T	Penn State	0–0	A	20,000
Nov. 14	W	Carnegie Tech	26–0	H	27,000
Nov. 21	W	Northwestern	13–10	H	27,000
Nov. 26	L	Nebraska	0–17	A	45,000
			200–64		278,000

1926

(9–1–0)
Co-Captains: Eugene Edwards
and Thomas Hearden

Oct. 2	W	Beloit	77–0	H	8,000
Oct. 9	W	Minnesota	20–7	A	c48,648
Oct. 16	W	Penn State	28–0	H	18,000
Oct. 23	W	Northwestern	6–0	A	41,000
Oct. 30	W	Georgia Tech	12–0	H	11,000
Nov. 6	W	Indiana	26–0	H	20,000
Nov. 13	W	Army	7–0	YS	63,029
Nov. 20	W	Drake	21–0	H	20,000
Nov. 27	L	Carnegie Tech	0–19	A	45,000
Dec. 4	W	So. Calif.	13–12	A	74,378
			210–38		349,055

1927

(7–1–1)
Captain: John P. Smith

Oct. 1	W	Coe	28–7	H	10,000
Oct. 8	W	Detroit	20–0	A	28,000
Oct. 15	W	Navy	19–6	N1	45,101
Oct. 22	W	Indiana	19–6	A	16,000
Oct. 29	W	Georgia Tech	26–7	H	17,000
Nov. 5	T	Minnesota	7–7	H	25,000
Nov. 12	L	Army	0–18	YS	65,678
Nov. 19	W	Drake	32–0	A	8,412
Nov. 26	W	So. California	7–6	N2*	120,000
			158–57		335,191

*Paid attendance: 99,573
N1 — at Baltimore; N2 — at Soldier Fied

1928

(5–4–0)
Captain: Frederick Miller

Sep. 29	W	Loyola (N.O.)	12–6	A	15,000
Oct. 6	L	Wisconsin	6–22	A	29,885
Oct. 13	W	Navy	7–0	N1*	120,000
Oct. 20	L	Georgia Tech	0–13	A	35,000
Oct. 27	W	Drake	32–6	H	12,000
Nov. 3	W	Penn State	9–0	N2	30,000
Nov. 10	W	Army	12–6	YS	78,188
Nov. 17	L	Carnegie Tech	7–27	N†	27,000
Dec. 1	L	So. California	14–27	A	72,632
			99–107		419,705

*Paid attendance: 103,081
†First defeat at home since 1905
N1 — at Soldier Field: N2 — at Philadelphia

1929†

(9–0–0)
Captain: John Law

Oct. 5	W	Indiana	14–0	A	16,111
Oct. 12	W	Navy	14–7	N1	64,681
Oct. 19	W	Wisconsin	19–0	N2	90,000
Oct. 26	W	Carnegie Tech	7–0	A	66,000
Nov. 2	W	Georgia Tech	26–6	A	22,000
Nov. 9	W	Drake	19–7	N2	50,000
Nov. 16	W	So. California	13–12	N2*	112,912
Nov. 23	W	Northwestern	26–6	A	c50,000
Nov. 30	W	Army	7–0	YS	79,408
			145–38		551,112

†No home games; Notre Dame Stadium was under construction
*Paid attendance: 99,351
N1 — at Baltimore; N2 — at Soldier Field

1930

(10–0–0)
Captain: Thomas Conley

Oct. 4	W S.M.U.	20–14	H	14,751
Oct. 11	W Navy†	26–2	H	40,593
Oct. 18	W Carnegie Tech	21–6	H	30,009
Oct. 25	W Pittsburgh	35–19	A	66,586
Nov. 1	W Indiana	27–0	H	11,113
Nov. 8	W Pennsylvania	60–20	A	75,657
Nov. 15	W Drake	28–7	H	10,106
Nov. 22	W Northwestern	14–0	A	44,648
Nov. 29	W Army	7–6	N1*	110,000
Dec. 6	W So. California	27–0	A	73,967
		265–74		477,430

†Dedication of Notre Dame Stadium
*Paid attendance: 103,310
N1 — at Soldier Field

APPENDIX C

ROCKNE'S ASSISTANT COACHES

Listed below are the individuals who served as assistant football coaches at Notre Dame during the head-coaching tenure of Knute Rockne.

Heartley (Hunk) Anderson	1924-27, 1930
Jack Chevigny	1929-30
Gus Dorais	1919
Walter Halas	1920-21
Tom Lieb	1924-25, 1929
Tommy Mills	1927-28
John P. Smith	1928
John (Ike) Voedisch	1929-30

APPENDIX D

ROCKNE'S PLAYERS

Listed below are the names of all of the young men who played in at least one play in a varsity football game at Notre Dame during the head-coaching tenure of Knute Rockne.

A

Ed Agnew	1930
John Ambrose	1919
Eddie Anderson	1918-21
Heartley (Hunk) Anderson	1918-21
Russ Arndt	1922-24

B

Joe Bach	1923-24
Leonard (Pete) Bahan	1918-19
Roy Bailie	1929-30
George Barry	1923
Norm Barry	1918-20
Joe Benda	1925-27
Arthur (Dutch) Bergman	1919
Joe (Dutch) Bergman	1921-23
Art Boeringer	1925-26
Joe Boland	1924-26
Gus Bondi	1927-29
Jim Brady	1927-28
Joe Brandy	1919-20
Jim Bray	1926-28
Marty Brill	1929-30
Frank Brown	1926
Harvey Brown	1921-23
Frank Butler	1930
Bill Byrne	1926
John Byrne	1921
Tom Byrne	1925-27

C

Alexander Cameron	1921
Jack Cannon	1927-29
Glen (Judge) Carberry	1920-22
Frank Carideo	1928-30
James Carmody	1930
Bill Cassidy	1929
Paul Castner	1920-22
Vince Cavanaugh	1930
Bill Cerney	1922-24
Jack Chevigny	1926-28
Norb Christman	1928-30
Francis Cody	1925
Maurice (Pat) Cohen	1926
Chuck Collins	1922-24
Eddie Collins	1926-29
Fred Collins	1925-28
John Colrick	1927-29
Tom Conley	1928-30
Ward Connell	1922-24
Ben Connors	1918-19
Harold Cook	1922
Forrest Cotton	1920-22
Bernie Coughlin	1922, 24-25
Danny Coughlin	1920-21
Frank Coughlin	1919-20
Carl Cronin	1929-30
Clem Crowe	1923-25
Ed Crowe	1925
Charlie Crowley	1918-19
Jim Crowley	1922-24
Al Culver	1929-30

D

Ray (Bucky) Dahman	1925-27
Walter DeGree	1919-22
Art Denchfield	1927
Gus Desch	1921-22
Billy Dew	1927-28

Joe Dienhart	1924
John Doarn	1926-28
Dick Donoghue	1927-30
Red Donovan	1918
Jim Dooley	1919-21
William Drennan	1922

E

Wilbur Eaton	1923-24
Gene (Red) Edwards	1924-26
Joe Eggeman	1923
Herb Eggert	1924
Jack Elder	1927-29
Rex Enright	1923, 25

F

Tom Farrell	1923
Norm Feltes	1922
Joe Fiske	1923
Bill Fitzpatrick	1926
Christie Flanagan	1925-27
Neil Flinn	1922
Jack Flynn	1921-22
Joe Foley	1930
John Frederick	1925-27
George Fitzpatrick	1919

G

Art (Hector) Garvey	1920-21
Al Gebert	1928-29
Oswald Geniesse	1924
George Gipp	1917-20
Charles Glueckert	1922-24
Hank Grabner	1918
Chet Grant	1920-21
Norm Greeney	1930

H

Dick Hanley	1930
Dick Hanousek	1924-25
Joe Harmon	1923-24
Russ Harmon	1922
Vince Harrington	1922-24
Jim Harris	1930
Dave Hayes	1919-20
Tom Hearden	1924-26
Norm Herwit	1928
Joe Higi	1921
Frank (Nordy) Hoffman	1930
John Hogan	1926
Paul Hogan	1918
Barny Holton	1920
Paul Host	1930
Max Houser	1923-24
Al Howard	1929-30
Ed Hunsinger	1922-24
Jim Hurlbert	1926-27
Bill Hurley	1926-27

J

Johnny James	1922
Chuck Jaskwhich	1930
Bill Jones	1926-27

K

Mickey Kane	1920-22
Clarence Kaplan	1929-30
Cy Kasper	1919-20
Tom Kassis	1928-30
Frank Keefe	1926
Larry Keefe	1924
Tommy Kenneally	1927-29
Frank Kersjes	1930

Roger Kiley	1919-21	Gene Mayl	1921-23
Bennie Kirk	1918-19	Vince McAdams	1926
Noble Kizer	1922-24	Harold McCabe	1925-26
Mike Koken	1930	Frank McCarthy	1927
Ed Kosky	1930	Frank McDermott	1921
Dave Krembs	1927	Frank McGrath	1923
Joe Kurth	1930	Jack McGrath	1926-28
		Charles McKinney	1926-27
L		Art McManmon	1929-30
		John McManmon	1924-26
Clarence LaFollette	1923	John McMullan	1923-25
Earl (Curly) Lambeau	1918	Vince McNally	1925-26
Fred (Ojay) Larson	1918-21	Regis McNamara	1929-30
John Law	1926-29	Paul McNulty	1922
Elmer Layden	1922-24	John McSorley	1926-27
Bernie Leahy	1929-30	Harry Mehre	1919-21
Frank Leahy	1928-30	Bert Metzger	1928-30
George Leppig	1926-28	Frank Milbauer	1922-23
Tom Lieb	1921-22	Frank Miles	1918
Tom Listzwan	1928	Don Miller	1922-24
Bernie Livergood	1922-24	Earl Miller	1918
Frank (Abbie) Lockard	1918	Edgar (Rip) Miller	1922-24
Joe Locke	1927, 29	Fred Miller	1926-28
Les Logan	1920-22	Gerry Miller	1922-24
Camilo Lombardo	1918	Howard Miller	1921
Nick Lukats	1930	Walter Miller	1919
		Les Mixon	1922
M		Johnny Mohardt	1918-21
		Bill Mohn	1918
Edward (Slip) Madigan	1919	Jack Montroy	1928
Hugh Magevney	1921	Dan Moore	1925-26
Willie Maher	1921-23	Joe Morrissey	1926-28
Dick Mahoney	1930	Tim Moynihan	1926-29
Gene Mahoney	1927	Larry (Moon) Mullins	1927-30
Grover Malone	1919	Emmett Murphy	1930
Ray Marelli	1925-26	Gene Murphy	1921-22
Bob Massey	1930	Tim Murphy	1921-23
Joe Maxwell	1924-26	Tom Murphy	1927-29
Frank Mayer	1925-26		

N

Romanus Nadolney	1918
Joe Nash	1926-29
John Nichols	1930
John Niemiec	1926-28
Tom Noon	1926
John Noppenberger	1923

O

Gene Oberst	1920, 22-23
Harry O'Boyle	1924-26
Tom O'Boyle	1924
Johnny O'Brien	1928-30
Paul (Bucky) O'Connor	1928-30
George O'Hara	1919
Tom Owen	1918

P

Art Parisien	1925-26
Dudley Pearson	1919
Bob Phelan	1919-21
John Phillips	1918
Bill Pierce	1930
John Polinsky	1925-27
Joe Prelli	1924-25, 27
George Prokop	1918-20
John Provissiero	1928

Q

Jim Quinn	1926

R

Jerry Ransavage	1926-28
Bob Reagan	1921-23
Joe Reedy	1925

Frank Reese	1921, 23-24
Clarence Reilly	1924
Jack Reilly	1928
Joe Rigali	1924-25
Charlie Riley	1925-27
John Roach	1923-26
John Rogers	1930
John Ruckelshaus	1925

S

Cy Sanders	1918-19
Joe Savoldi	1928-30
Eddie Scharer	1924-25
Herb Schultz	1927
Charles Schwartz	1929
Marchy Schwartz	1929-30
Frank Seyfrit	1920-21
George Shanahan	1918
Rodney Shaughnessy	1921
George Shaw	1927-29
Lawrence (Buck) Shaw	1919-21
Bill Shea	1920-21
Joe Sheeketski	1930
Bob Shields	1926
Fred Slackford	1919
Dick Smith	1925-26
Fred Smith	1921
Howard Smith	1927
John (Clipper) Smith	1925-27
Maurice (Clipper) Smith	1918-20
Fred Staab	1930
Gus Stange	1922-23
Alfred Stepan	1928
Raleigh (Rollo) Stine	1918
Harry Stuhldreher	1922-24

T

Bob Terlack	1930
Frank Thomas	1920-22
George Trafton	1919
Cliff Trombley	1925
Ted Twomey	1928-29

V

Bill Van Roso	1930
George Vergara	1922-23
Manny Vezie	1926-29
George Vlk	1928-30
John (Ike) Voedisch	1925-27
Bill Voss	1920-22

W

John Wallace	1923-26
Adam Walsh	1922-24
Charles Walsh	1925-27
Earl Walsh	1919-21
John Weibel	1922-24
Jim Whelan	1925
Eddie White	1925, 27
Richard White	1918
Percy Wilcox	1920
Bo Williams	1928
Chet Wynne	1918-21
Elmer Wynne	1925-27

Y

Tommy Yarr	1929-30

ABOUT THE EDITORS

Robert Quakenbush

Robert A. Quakenbush is president of Robert Quakenbush Public Relations, an independent public relations firm located in Chicago.

His first book, THE GIPPER'S GHOST, told the entertaining and inspiring story of a winless, down-on-its-luck Fighting Irish football team that finally returns to glory when its Number One Fan — God Almighty — sends Knute Rockne and The Gipper back to South Bend to resurrect Notre Dame's winning tradition.

Bob received his bachelor's degree in management from Notre Dame, and earned his M.B.A. from Ball State University in Muncie, Indiana.

An active member of the Notre Dame Club of Chicago, Bob once served as chairman of the Club's annual Knute Rockne Awards Dinner.

Mike Bynum

Mike Bynum is one of the South's most successful young authors. He is the author of seven previous books, all based on football, including BEAR BRYANT'S BOYS OF AUTUMN, AGGIE PRIDE and, with Steadman Shealy, NEVER SAY QUIT, considered by many to be one of the finest inspirational books for young people ever written. Adding to his list of credits, Mike served as consulting producer to the Mizlou TV special, BEAR BRYANT — COUNTDOWN TO 315, which was produced for NBC.

A former student manager for Coach Bryant's Crimson Tide football team and honor student at The University of Alabama, Mike is completing a trilogy of football's three greatest coaches — Bryant, Rockne and Lombardi — after which he will be attending law school.